Additional Praise for
Civic Work, Civic Lessons

"I am struck by the unique gift this book offers readers, two distinctly different yet equally valuable perspectives on public service. What a blessing for Ernestine Fu to be able to have Tom Ehrlich as a mentor, and how incredibly invigorating it must have been for Tom Ehrlich to work with Ernestine Fu, who seems destined to do great things."–**John Merrow**, Education Correspondent, PBS NewsHour; President, Learning Matters, Inc.

"Through this inter-generational approach, *Civic Work, Civic Lessons* brings together two unique perspectives about remarkable experiences in public service. Tom Ehrlich and Ernestine Fu lead by example, demonstrating the value of civic engagement in the private and public sectors and challenging us to expand our personal civic efforts."–**Maureen F. Curley**, President, Campus Compact

"We can either inspire hope and optimism for the next generation by engaging them in the process to rebuild the public and private sector, or we can leave them behind. Tom Ehrlich and Ernestine Fu's honest discussion of so many difficult issues — sharing examples of failure and success — takes immense courage and vision to inspire greater good. I am inspired!"–**Kim Meredith**, Executive Director, Center on Philanthropy and Civil Society at Stanford University

"The Stanford community has a long history of public service. This book — written by members of two different generations of the Stanford family, Tom Ehrlich, a faculty member, and Ernestine Fu, a student — is very much in our university's spirit. It explores the importance and relevance of service in its many forms and the benefits that come when generations reach out to each other. It offers valuable insights for tomorrow's leaders."–**John Hennessy**, President, Stanford University

CIVIC WORK, CIVIC LESSONS

Two Generations Reflect on Public Service

Thomas Ehrlich and Ernestine Fu

University Press of America,® Inc.
Lanham • Boulder • New York • Toronto • Plymouth, UK

Copyright © 2013 by University Press of America,® Inc.
An imprint of the Rowman & Littlefield Publishing Group
4501 Forbes Boulevard, Suite 200, Lanham, Maryland 20706
UPA Aquisitions Department (301) 459-3366

10 Thornbury Road, Plymouth PL6 7PP, United Kingdom

Library of Congress Control Number: 2013936288
ISBN: 978-0-7618-6127-0 (paperback : alk. paper)—ISBN: 978-0-7618-6128-7
(electronic)

∞™ The paper used in this publication meets the minimum requirements of
American National Standard for Information Sciences Permanence of Paper
for Printed Library Materials, ANSI/NISO Z39.48-1992.

For Ellen, with love from Tom

For Christine, with love from Ernestine

CONTENTS

FOREWORD
BY BILL DRAYTON, CEO,
ASHOKA: INNOVATORS FOR THE PUBLIC

In elementary school, I could not imagine any useful reason why I was being tortured by Latin and math. Nor was I much more enthusiastic about being a crashee in soccer. However, I was fascinated by how the world works and I loved starting things, especially newspapers.

Once I had saved enough to buy a mimeograph machine (thereby escaping the production technology of typing very hard so that the fifth carbon copy could be read), I was unstoppable. As the paper grew to 30 and then 50 pages, and as it reached well beyond my school and required more and more advertisers, I did what was obviously necessary, even though that meant that I was not always where I should have been.

Many years later when my mother died, I found correspondence between her and my school's principal. She was concerned. (Why is my fifth-grader neither in school or at home?). The principal patiently kept advising everyone to trust me — and not to show they were anxious. Bless him! Just as Tom Ehrlich and Ernestine Fu benefited from wonderful early mentors (Lesson 1), in retrospect, I know that this act of invisible mentoring was a magic carpet that opened the way to a life of always being able to give and therefore never having to be afraid. Each of the Lessons Tom and Ernestine tell us, with wonderful stories to illustrate those Lessons, are paths to guide young people on the road to being effective changemakers.

Once a young person has had this experience of having a dream, building a team, and changing his or her world, he or she has the power to express love and respect in significant action. Nothing is more important for happiness, health, and longevity. He or she will be a changemaker for life. Each success is so deeply satisfying that it leads on to the next. And each new undertaking builds the changemaker's skills and confidence. And once you know you can change the world, no one can ever take that power from you. You sense this when Ernestine describes her experience launching Visual Arts and Music for Society at 15 and how central it has become for her.

We know where this leads. It is not accidental that over 80 percent of the over 3,000 leading social entrepreneur Ashoka Fellows started something in their teens, usually their early teens. More than half have changed national policy, as Tom has done, and three quarters the pattern in their field at the national level, within five years of their launch.

If you want to be a great social entrepreneur, the earlier you give yourself permission to start changing the world, the better. This has always been true. What is different now is that *everyone* in this generation of children and young people *must* master the complex underlying skills required for changemaking and know they are changemakers before they turn 21. *Everyone.* Not just everyone in the elite, which sufficed even a generation or so ago.

Why this sudden, fundamental shift? A simple mathematical fact: The rate of change has been escalating exponentially for at least three centuries.

This central historical fact has now reached the point that the way we humans have organized ourselves and therefore also the social skills we have had to have to succeed are failing — ever faster and ever more broadly. The death rate of the biggest U.S. businesses has been accelerating for 40 years. Income distributions worldwide are widening as demand for the bottom 20 to 70 percent of different societies without these new skills collapses, even as there are urgent bidding wars for the few with excellent changemaking skills. Corruption flourishes as accelerating change and complexity render the old rules and punishment systems increasingly useless.

There has always been change, at least evolutionary change. Over the 50,000 years since humans crossed the mouth of the Red Sea, our skulls have become progressively thinner as we have learned to cooperate. Then, as homo sapiens left Africa, the largest groups they could organize had 100 to 150 members. Now we have billion-person countries and the World Wide Web.

However, from the perspective of a human life, change was too slow and narrowly episodic to be the focus. Instead the goal for organization has been efficiency in repetition. Think the assembly line and the law firm. This has meant a few people telling others how to repeat together like clockwork — a system characterized by vertical nervous systems and walls. And an educational system designed to fit.

Now, however, as the rate of change continues to accelerate, the world is quickly moving to the opposite paradigm. For millennia, the pieces have fitted together as repetition reinforced repetition. Now, as each piece changes and bumps the pieces it touches, which then bump all the pieces they touch, *change begets and accelerates change.*

Now every group must become an open, fluid, team of teams to survive. Open because most ideas and resources are outside. Fluid because "the client" is a kaleidoscope of changing elements and success requires assembling ever-changing teams of teams to be able to serve well. Teams because the group needs everyone to be scanning for opportunities to serve and skilled at delivering change.

In this world, no one can afford people who are not skilled as changemakers on their team. Now, young children must master and practice a high level of cognitive empathy. Any person who fails to do so will be cruelly and quickly marginalized.

Why? Because as change accelerates, the rules cover less and less. They haven't been invented yet, or they are in conflict. No matter how diligently a person tries to follow the rules, without empathy, they *will* hurt people and disrupt groups — and they *will* be thrown out.

When the brain rewires and children become young people, around 12, they must become changemakers and practice the four key skills required — empathy, teamwork, a very new form of leadership, and changemaking — in action. That's why my newspaper and Ernestine's arts service program were so important. This book will help you map how to do so, but ultimately the only way to become a changemaker is to be one.

We can see the early beachheads of this new world all around us, be it the Jesuits or Google, Silicon Valley or the emergence and explosive growth of social entrepreneurship over the last 33 years.

Once we get past the mess of the transition, this is a far, far better world than what we have had before:

- With everyone an intelligent, caring changemaker, there is no way the problems can outrun the solutions.
- With everyone both (a) guided by empathy-based ethics and (b) leading as powerful changemakers, we will have an at-its-root far more equal and therefore fair society.
- Everyone, not just the one percent, will be able to contribute, to express love and respect in action — the ultimate elixir of happiness and well-being.

The foundation of all this ultimately rests on us all developing a very high level of empathy-based ethics. Without this, forget teamwork / new leadership / changemaking. Without this, individuals will be thrown out and society rendered dysfunctional.

Guided by this compass to our North Star, human society is now fast and irreversibly making the leap to the next level in our long historical evolution to become both far more independent and far more social.

We must all become social changemakers working for the good of all. Tom Ehrlich and Ernestine Fu provide wise counsel to achieve that goal.

INTRODUCTION
Co-Authors 57 Years Apart

More than 57 years in age separate us—Tom Ehrlich and Ernestine Fu. One might reasonably ask why we thought that we should collaborate on a book designed to be of interest to readers of all ages, and particularly to young people considering a commitment of their time and talent to helping others in their community, whether that community is local, state, national, or international.

The book initially began because Tom wanted to chronicle ways in which his life has been enriched by public service as both a vocation and an avocation, with the aim of encouraging young people to be active civically. Tom wrote a rough draft telling that story. But it was clear to reviewers of the draft that it could not meet the goal of encouraging youth civic engagement unless it included lessons learned from young civic activists. Fortunately, Tom was put in touch with Ernestine, a Stanford University undergraduate who he thought epitomized the characteristics of mind and heart that he has sought to promote. Ernestine brings to the partnership a rich background of experience herself, as will become clear in this volume, as well as contacts with scores of young people who are also engaged in civic projects and have shared with us their own insights and understandings.

This book results from the extended conversations that Ernestine and Tom have had concerning the goal of civic engagement. We believe that our democracy requires men and women of all ages and all walks of life to find their own civic paths and to pursue them with determination, compassion, respect for others, and humility about the limitations of their own perspectives. The chapters that follow emphasize seven key lessons that we stress are central to promoting that goal. Each chapter includes two sections, one written by Tom and the other by Ernestine. A final chapter focuses on new ways to leverage technology for civic engagement.

Most of the civic work that Tom has done involved public-policy positions in government. Ernestine's civic work has primarily been in starting her own nonprofit organization, helping finance social enterprises, and engaging in a wide range of other civic organizations. Although the paths we have taken differ, reflecting the differences in our particular interests as well as our ages, we are similar in the passion we each bring to our civic work. We both find that our civic work has become part of our identities, part of who we are as human beings. That work has enabled us both to feel connected to something larger than ourselves and to the world around us in ways that would not have happened without our commitment to public service. While we each take on new civic ventures from time to time, and leave others when it seems right to do so, the call to public service to which we have each responded to in our own ways is always with us. We both believe that people of all ages can find enormous satisfaction in civic work, just as we have.

Civic work can take a wide range of different forms. Some of those forms are focused on helping others by providing assistance that fellow human beings require and are entitled to—food, medical care, education, or other basic needs. We never think of this kind of work as "charity," but rather as collaborating with others because our efforts not only help others, but also enrich ourselves, and bring us satisfaction, a sense of accomplishment, and connection with the world around us. Some of this civic work is part-time, as avocations that we do along with our vocational positions. Ernestine's civic work has naturally followed this path since she is still a full-time student. Much of Tom's civic work, on the other hand, has been full-time, primarily in the federal government, though he has also participated in many nonprofit civic organizations. These varied experiences of ours, and those with whom we have connected through our common commitment to civic work, provide the basis for the stories in this book and the lessons we draw from those stories. We hope the insights that our readers—particularly young people, and those who counsel them—draw from the pages that follow will encourage them to find their own civic passions and to translate those passions into action.

But first we should each introduce ourselves.

TOM

It was a fall day in 1963. The scene was a drab auditorium in the Department of State in Washington, D.C. The room was packed with those designated as "senior officials," and I had the good fortune to be one of them, though I was only a 29-year old special assistant to Under Secretary of State George W. Ball.

We all stood as President John F. Kennedy walked into the room and up to the podium. I do not recall the exact words he spoke that day, but I do remember that he began by thanking us for our civic work and that he spoke eloquently about the importance of that work. I felt he was talking directly to me and remember also that I felt 10-feet tall as I listened to his brief remarks.

I was part of the Kennedy administration, and subsequent administrations thereafter of Presidents Johnson, Ford, Carter, and Clinton, in part because I had been stirred by Kennedy and his call for those like me to ask ourselves "not what your country can do for you, but what you can do for your country." In the years since then, I have come to believe even more deeply in the value of civic work, value to those who engage in the work no less than to the government and its citizenry. And I have come to realize that civic education is essential for all our citizens, whether or not they choose civic work as careers or rather make that work an avocation by becoming civic leaders in their communities. I have learned that civic knowledge, skills, and dispositions can and should be taught to ensure that our democracy functions as it should.

My exposure to public service began at the outset of World War II, when I was eight years old and my father joined the federal government in the Office of Price Administration and our family moved to Washington, D.C. I did not understand much about what my father was doing—helping to prevent price gouging while scarce goods and supplies that might otherwise be available for domestic consumers were funneled to the war effort. But I knew that he was part of the huge public undertaking by the United States and its allies to protect our freedoms. As I write this, I am looking at a wartime poster that my uncle, a U.S. civil servant all his life, created to help ensure that Americans knew what we were fighting for: "The world cannot exist half slave and half free," it says. "Work for freedom!"

I grew up in a time when most Americans shared a strong sense of civic responsibility. This was an era when adults who had lived through the New Deal and World War II recognized the importance of civic work to the preservation of both their physical and economic security. Almost all of them had experienced sacrifices during this period. Many had served in the armed forces during the War, and everyone knew someone who was killed or whose relative died then. The War galvanized civilians to assist their country and to accept food and fuel rationing and other limitations on their daily lives. At the same time, Americans generally believed they had a responsibility to make our democracy work well by participating in its processes, by engaging in what Ernestine and I term civic work.

As I'll describe in the pages that follow, I've had the good fortune to be guided by splendid mentors who modeled civic work in different arenas. And I have been privileged to engage myself in a range of full-time and part-time positions in government and in the nonprofit world of civic work. Inevitably, however, when someone my age—78 as I write these words—describes career challenges and choices, it is tempting to ignore two key dimensions of the full-disclosure picture. One is all the positions that I applied for, but failed to be chosen. Over the last five decades, I was runner-up for a number of public-service jobs that I might well have taken had I been selected and, if I had, my own life and that of my family could have been very different. Several times when I was not chosen I felt as though I had "failed." Today, looking back, it seems that for every door that was closed, not much time passed before another opened. Most often, they opened through a combination of my own efforts and those of others. In the latter part of the 1970s, for example, I really wanted to work directly for President Carter, and was not chosen for several such positions. But then Warren Christopher, the Deputy Secretary of State and a close friend for more than a decade, proposed me as the head of a new agency reporting to the President and having responsibility for both bilateral and multi-lateral U.S. foreign-aid policies.

The second and much more important dimension is my family and friends. The greatest blessing of my life has been to be married to my wife, Ellen. Over the course of more than 55 years together we have each engaged in civic work, and I have learned much from her insights. We met as undergraduates. Ellen was a Radcliffe student, and I was at Harvard, during the time when Radcliffe and Harvard were separate institutions but the students took all their classes together. She and I were both in the Class of 1956, and we were both Government majors. We started dating in our junior year and by our senior year we had definite plans to be married. After graduating from Radcliffe, Ellen worked to support us as a research assistant and then as a fifth-grade teacher. While our three children were very young, she devoted full-time to raising them, but in subsequent years she also worked as a fund-raiser for a program at Georgetown University, for the National Portrait Gallery in Washington, and for Planned Parenthood in Philadelphia. She has been a trustee of Radcliffe College and has been an active volunteer as well as a board member for Abilities United, an organization in Palo Alto, California, helping people with disabilities. While Ellen and I were in Indiana, she was an extraordinarily active leader of civic causes. She chaired the United Way of the county where Indiana University Bloomington is located and was a tireless advocate for civic organizations in this role. This work led to her being chosen as a member of the United Way of American Board of Governors, which she helped to guide through one of its most difficult periods. When we left Indiana University, the Trustees gave Ellen unprecedented recognition by the award of an honorary degree, citing her "as a splendid exemplar of public service for the enhancement of community life," one who "brightened countless lives with her enthusiasm, energy, and warmth." Most of my stories are from my own life, rather than Ellen's, because I know my stories first-hand. But she could tell her own remarkable tales of her civic work, of which I am enormously proud.

No one who came of age in the era that I did could have then imagined what has become commonplace in recent decades: politicians campaigning against Washington in their efforts to gain the presidency or a seat in Congress. We knew first-hand, or at least from our parents, that the country's future totally depended on the abilities of the federal government to protect its citizenry and on the willingness of the citizenry to support that government. Civic work, whether in the military or in civilian service, was viewed as noble work.

Over the last fifty years I have held six full-time jobs in government: speech-writer for the Governor of Massachusetts, Foster Furcolo; law clerk for Judge Learned Hand of the U.S. Second Circuit Court of Appeals; special assistant to the Legal Adviser to the State Department, Abram Chayes, in the Kennedy and Johnson administrations; special assistant to the Under Secretary of State, George W. Ball, in the Johnson administration; president of the Legal Services Corporation, subject to a Board of Directors chosen initially by the President Ford and then by President Carter, and approved by Congress; and director of the International Development Cooperation Agency, chosen and reporting directly to President Carter after the U.S. Senate approved my appointment.

The rest of my full-time professional life has been working in universities. My early years in education were as a faculty member and administrator at Stanford University, where I was first a professor and then the dean of the Law School. Later I was provost at the University of Pennsylvania. I consciously chose to move from Penn to a public institution, Indiana University, because I wanted to grapple with the issues of public access to higher education as well as ones of quality.

On a part-time basis, I have also served in a number of federal-government roles. My first started when I was still a student at Harvard College when I joined the U.S. Army Reserve, where I was an enlisted soldier for six years. Much later in life I served on a Commission on Military Compensation, appointed by President Carter and charged with revising the military retirement program. In addition, I was appointed by President George H. W. Bush to the Commission on National and Community Service (and was later chair of that Commission), and I was then appointed and reappointed by President Clinton to the Board of Directors of the Commission's successor organization, the Corporation on National and Community Service. These appointments all required confirmation by the U.S. Senate.

In this book, as Ernestine and I indicate, our definition of civic work includes assisting nonprofit organizations as well as working in a government position. While dean at Stanford Law School, provost at the University of Pennsylvania, and then president at Indiana University, I served on the boards of a number of national educational organizations, and these roles helped me do a better job as an administrator while giving me an opportunity to serve higher education and the public. I have also been a trustee of Bennett College, a historically Black college for women, of the University of Pennsylvania, and of Mills College, as well as chair of various higher-education organizations.

The organization that has given me the greatest satisfaction is called Campus Compact, which now has the presidents of almost 1200 colleges and universities as its members and has 34 state affiliates. It was founded, with the help of one of my mentors, John W. Gardner, to encourage college students to engage as volunteers in civic work in their communities. My daughter, Elizabeth, who was one of the very first employees of Campus Compact, helped me understand how critical it is for college and university presidents to speak out about public service and to facilitate ways in which students can participate.

ERNESTINE

Wedged in the back pocket of my wallet, hugging the business card I made when I was ten-years old, is a photo of my sister and me that always brings back mixed memories. We are adorned in matching blue-striped collared shirts with white denim shorts and embracing one another—a loving, yet previously rare sight. Like many siblings, Christine and I fought constantly. From who hit the tennis ball harder to who multiplied numbers more quickly, we were two hard-driving over-achievers, competing for awards and recognition. Our rivalry came to a quick halt when Christine was diagnosed with depression. Despite all our squabbles, I still loved my sister deeply. Even though she had doctors, psychologists, mentors, and medications, I kept asking myself, "What can I do for her?"

I started encouraging her to play the flute with me, and slowly saw our common interest in music take on a therapeutic role. We began with *Selected Duets for Flutes* and moved on to more advanced pieces in Friedrich Kuhlau's *Three Duos Brilliants*. Initially, our disharmony was audible, but after days and weeks of practice and communication, a mellifluous sound began to emerge. Our relationship transformed from one of sibling rivalries to that of an integrated team: two sisters with one musical voice and sound.

As I visited the hospital to see my sister, I realized that even among my peers and community, there were many people just like her. This insight and the moments leading up to it became the factors driving my decision to engage in civic work. I wanted to do for others what flute duets had done for us, and also help Christine feel a sense of duty and responsibility—that there was a reason to live and that she was not just a "person in need."

With Christine's help, I started a nonprofit organization to share the power of music. Through Visual Arts and Music for Society, I encouraged fellow high-school artists and musicians to use their talents to organize events for people in need. Our audience included abused women, homeless families, orphans, and senior citizens. As the organization quickly expanded, these people in the community became a part of who I am. Instead of writing a check for charity, it allowed me to develop one-on-one connections with people in need, as I had with my sister. I reached out to others, strangers suffering from different mental and physical disorders, and these people in turn defined and shaped me. As I sought to make musical ensembles an engaging, regular part of their lives, the people I was helping opened my eyes to a deeper sense of personal satisfaction, beyond collecting trophies and awards.

This initiative pushed me to immerse myself in a range of civic ventures that other young people were engaged in throughout the country. The summer before college, I joined a national board responsible for allocating corporate philanthropy dollars to youth civic causes. I witnessed firsthand how a private corporation could alleviate social problems. While I was inspired to learn about other ways in which the private sector could positively impact the public sector and help further social causes, I never imagined myself involved in the day-to-day activities of the private sector.

During the financial crisis in 2008 and subsequent global recession, my dad was laid off from J.P. Morgan Chase in 2009. He has worked for twenty years as a computer programmer, starting at Great Western Bank, to its acquisition by Washington Mutual Bank, and subsequently by J.P. Morgan Chase. I was looking for a job to help fund my undergraduate tuition at Stanford. It was then that I immersed myself in the Silicon Valley entrepreneurship culture surrounding the University and joined a venture-capital firm. I identified my first investment within two months of joining the firm, convinced the partners to fund an early-stage technology company, and then collaborated with an attorney from a leading Silicon Valley law firm to negotiate with the entrepreneurs. It was a bewildering and lengthy process. I was nineteen when the investment process began, and twenty when the deal closed. My experiences during the time sparked a keen interest in how the private sector could draw on cutting-edge research and rapidly deploy new technologies to improve society's quality of life. The skills and insights that I gained through my investment, and subsequent experiences at the firm, also directly benefited my ability to do effective civic work, for much of the learning I acquired also had direct application to social entrepreneurship, and more broadly, to a range of different kinds of civic work.

My call to public service also led me to study global environmental challenges at the School of Engineering. I examined the ability of a coastal-area infrastructure to adapt to sea-level rise produced by climate change and technology to efficiently power our energy needs. I had the opportunity to put my studies into practice when I joined Stanford's Board of Trustees as a student representative and member of its Committee on Land and Buildings, where the sustainability of Stanford's buildings was a critical component in our decision-making. I also directed the Student Services Division of student government, reviving a dying service branch that oversaw local sustainability as well as tutoring projects. I found great satisfaction in practicing these different forms of civic work.

Civic work, of course, has challenges. The nonprofit I had founded, for example, started out very modestly. It began when I co-founded its first local chapter at my high school and oversaw its activities and commitments as the club's president. Only six students attended our first meeting. Many times I thought the club would fail to meet its goals. A number of people supported me, however, and helped develop the nonprofit. My good friend Jasmine Schladen, for example, created the organization's website, in addition to attending every meeting. Many others assisted in my struggle to attract volunteers, complete stacks of government nonprofit-status forms, and hone my skills as a leader. This was my first lesson in coming to understand that every successful organization, whether for-profit or nonprofit, is indebted to great mentors and supporters. I mention some of my own great mentors in the first lesson of this book.

While Tom grew up in a time when most Americans shared a strong sense of civic responsibility, I grew up surrounded by the boom of the Internet and digital media. Technology has fundamentally changed the way we are able to interact with others in civic work, as we discuss in the last chapter. I have been able to use technology to connect with dozens of young civic leaders around the world, and in writing my portions of this book, I found it only natural to include their stories. Together, Tom and I interviewed them and tried our best to recreate their experiences as accurately as possible. These friends with whom I have collaborated in my civic work have been wise and compassionate leaders and serve as inspirations for what I hope to encourage in other youth.

TOM AND ERNESTINE

Most of the civic work that Ernestine discusses in illustrating our seven lessons is focused on nonprofit organizations like the one she has started. Most of the civic work that Tom talks about in these pages concern public service, particularly through the lenses of the various positions he held in the federal government. This difference is only natural since each of us has written about our own experiences and the experiences of those whom we know most closely.

Both of us believe passionately, however, that civic work—particularly by young people—in both the private and the public sectors is acutely needed, perhaps now more than ever before. In the year 2000, Professor Robert Putnam of Harvard wrote a seminal work titled *Bowling Alone: The Collapse and Revival of American Community* (Simon & Schuster, 2000). Putnam argued that Americans had become increasingly disconnected from each other in terms of the kinds of civic organizations that used to bind them together. He also pointed to the steady decline in political participation by each generation since World War II, as measured by traditional activities such as voting and other partisan activities including attending political rallies and working for political parties, as Tom had done. Putnam also noted that communal participation on matters of public policy, such as attending a public meeting or writing a letter to a magazine or newspaper, had declined as well. He stressed that this fraying of the American social fabric and loss of social capital was particularly acute among young people. All this suggested to Putnam a weakening in the civic health of our American society.

In the years since then, the story does not look much different in terms of involvement in politics and public policy. Youth political engagement has modestly increased, though not at the pace of their elders. But there has been an explosion of interest among young people in giving their time and energies, and what money they can spare, to promote literally tens of thousands of youth-led civic organizations like the one Ernestine founded as a teenager.

We are eager to see this youth energy not only continue to grow, but also to focus some of its attention on politics and public policy, just as we are eager to see the realm of public policy and politics learn from the civic work in which so many youth groups are now engaged. If our democracy is to flourish, youth must become much more active in public affairs, using the tools of digital media and other new technologies, as we outline in our last chapter.

Every generation has reshaped American civil society to meet the difficulties of its times. Although youth and those who counsel them are not our only intended audiences for this book, America's future depends on our youth, so young people are our primary focus. American youth today face particularly troubling challenges, both domestic and international. We are convinced that youth civic engagement can master those challenges. This was the basis for our judgment that each of us could contribute a distinct perspective on a troubling national need: To promote youth civic engagement far more widely and wisely than has been the case up to now. We hope our intergenerational vantage points offer useful insights for America's youth and for those who advise them.

LESSON I

Role Models, Mentors, and Teachers Are Key in Civic Work

TOM AND ERNESTINE

We start with the importance of mentors and teachers because they are usually the single most significant force in encouraging civic work, particularly among young people. Parents are often the first and most important of these mentors and teachers, and Tom's experiences, recounted in the pages that follow, are a prime example. Grandparents can serve in these capacities as well. Readers should particularly remember this reality, as they become parents and grandparents. Children look to these elders for the examples they set.

Take the deceptively simple issue of honesty. Too often, in our experience, parents cheat in small ways that are not lost on their children. They may tell a ticket-taker at a movie theater that their children are only age eleven in order to save on ticket prices. More commonly, they may violate the law by speeding in their cars. We do not suggest that any of us live our lives without sometimes behaving in unethical or even illegal ways along the lines of these two illustrations. But adults should bear in mind that children pay close attention to the misbehavior of those whose actions they are most often told to follow. If children become accustomed to an attitude of "do what I say, not what I do," in their parents or grandparents, the result will have a corrosive effect on the efforts of everyone else, in schools and beyond. It is essential to teach those children that integrity must be a fundamental precept of personal behavior, whether in the workplace, in school, in personal relations, or in civic life.

Engaging in civic work is also behavior that is best learned by modeling, and parents and grandparents are frequently the best models. At the same time, many civic leaders have not had the benefit of elders in their families who were role models of civic engagement. This need not be a barrier to learning how to engage in civic work. If a young person is lucky, she or he will be exposed to a teacher who becomes a mentor as well. Tom was fortunate, as his section reveals, that one of his law-school professors, Abram Chayes, asked him to become his special assistant in the Kennedy Administration, and Chayes became a superb mentor for Tom, as he tells in his section of this Lesson. Ernestine, on the other hand, reached out to one of the teachers in her high school, Chris Rodriguez, who was not someone she even knew personally. She took the initiative and sought the help of Mr. Rodriguez, and he had a pivotal influence on her civic work in building the nonprofit organization that she founded, as she describes in her section of this Lesson. Similarly, Tom would not have had the benefit of mentoring by Undersecretary of State George W. Ball if he had not first gone to Mr. Ball and asked him for a job, as he tells later in this book. And Ernestine would never have had an opportunity to work with partners in a venture capital firm unless she had reached out to them. Her time at that firm helped her develop empathetic insights about men and women from many different walks of life, and helped prepare her for the challenges of quickly building a large organization—strengths of Ernestine's she might not have had without her experience at that firm.

The stories in these pages should be read in the following light. Teachers and mentors may come into our lives uninvited, as our parents, our teachers, or in other capacities. But we can reach out to individuals whom we admire for the qualities of character and dedication they represent. Even if they do not necessarily seem to connect directly to civic work, as was true of Mr. Rodriguez, it may well turn out that they are role models to help us along on our journey toward engaging in that work.

TOM

My mother was my first civic role model and, by her example, my initial civic teacher. She had been trained as an architect at the University of Pennsylvania and M.I.T. But when she graduated in the middle of the Depression, there were no jobs available for architects, particularly women architects, and my mother went to work for the Fogg Art Museum at Harvard University, where she trained herself to be a restorer of art works on paper and, over time, an expert on art forgeries. She gained prominence in the field when she was working to restore a print of a famous engraving, "Battle of the Nudes," by the Italian Renaissance artist Pollaiuolo. The print had been given to the Museum by a celebrated benefactor who prided himself on his knowledge of art. When my mother was cleaning and repairing the print, she found that it was a fake. She made public her judgment even though this predictably angered the benefactor who was embarrassed to have been tricked by a forger. As a result, she put her role at the Museum at risk, but she also developed a reputation as a leading expert in the restoration of works on paper as well as in detecting forgeries.

During World War II, the original signed copy of the Declaration of Independence was moved from the National Archives in Washington, D.C., to Fort Knox, Tennessee, where the country's store of gold was kept. Sometime in 1943, those in charge of guarding the Declaration there noticed that it had developed a tear. They immediately became worried—or so the story goes as I was told it—that American citizens would fear there was a tear in the Republic that matched the tear in its founding document. In great secrecy, my mother was taken to Fort Knox, where she worked with colleagues to reweave the fibers and repair the tear. I knew this secret, and, being nine years old at the time, was brimming with civic pride. But I was not allowed to say a word about my mother's secret work to any of my friends.

Ten years later, in 1953, the country was torn by anti-Communist sentiments fueled by Senator Joseph McCarthy, who claimed that the State Department was riddled with secret Communist agents. A few years later, Richard Nixon made his reputation by echoing McCarthy's charges, and pointing to Alger Hiss as the top secret Soviet agent who worked in the State Department. Hiss denied the charges under oath, and was brought to trial for perjury. The key piece of evidence was the so-called "pumpkin papers" that an admitted former Communist, Whittaker Chambers, claimed to have received from Hiss after they were typed on Hiss's typewriter. Hiss was tried in 1949 and, after a hung jury, was tried again in 1950 and convicted.

As part of the appeal process, a lawyer for Hiss named Helen Buttenwieser, who was also an acquaintance of our family, asked my mother in 1952 to be an expert witness in the case and examine the "pumpkin papers" to try to determine whether they were typed on the Hiss typewriter. My mother agreed to do so in spite of the great potential jeopardy to her reputation by seeming to side with a man convicted of lying about his ties to Communism and the Soviet Union. FBI agents brought the documents to our apartment in Boston where my mother examined them. Ultimately, she concluded that they were forged, though the appeal by Hiss nonetheless failed. But the example that my mother set by doing what she saw as a civic duty in spite of very real dangers to her reputation made a lasting impression on me.

Hardly anyone is without some flaws, but these need not stop them from doing important civic work, or from inspiring others, and my mother was certainly no exception. She suffered from manic depression for years in the 1950s and 1960s, was an alcoholic during that period, and was probably clinically depressed well before then. She was treated several times in subsequent years at McLean Psychiatric Hospital outside of Boston, where she had electric-shock treatments. At least partially as a result of her illness, and through no fault of her own, she was a less than good mother to me and my sister. She had neither the temperament nor the energy to spend time as a parent. But she was a civic role model to me in that she seized opportunities to do civic work, and her example helped me to understand why doing so is important. In her work on the Hiss case, she faced the certainty that some of her friends would be critical that she helped the defense in a high-profile criminal case involving someone accused of treason whom she did not know. But she did it because she thought it was the right thing to do.

Civic mentors and teachers are so important because they can put a human face on what may otherwise seem an arid and abstract ideal of civic work. They can show how civic work can be done in a human way by those with multiple human weaknesses and illnesses, as was true of my mother. Even though she was terribly ill, she was able to teach me by her example.

Like my mother, my father was a civic role model for me, though he was of a very different, totally well-balanced sort. He worked for a year at the start of World War II in the federal Office of Price Administration in Washington, D.C., but our family came back to Boston in 1943, probably because my mother was too sick to be able to continue in Washington. Her dark moods made it increasingly difficult for friends of my parents to have any social time with them. Throughout those decades, my father did not complain or show less than complete love and caring support for my mother while he was also handling the household chores, paying the bills, and being father and mother to his two children. He never gave her or anyone else the sense that he was imposed upon and never apologized to others for her behavior or inactivity. His sensitive heart, his patience, and his unfailing kindness in his personal life always inspired me.

He was no less an inspiration in his civic roles, for he showed me by his example that civic engagement is a lifetime commitment. From the time we returned to Boston, he was engaged as a volunteer in a range of community organizations and activities to assist others. His vocation was part-ownership of a small chain of retail stores that sold women's clothes. But he was also always involved in helping several nonprofit organizations, some that served just our community and some that were national.

All my life, I adored my father. We were the closest of friends. We looked just alike, as my youngest son looks just like me and as my father looked just like my grandfather. A quartet of photographs hangs on the wall in our home with the caption, "Four generations of Ehrlich men at age 15"—my grandfather, my father, myself, and my son. We look like quadruplets, though the four generations span more than one hundred years. I never could imagine myself in the retail women's clothing business. It always struck me as both extremely difficult, with low profit margins and high risks of misjudging future fashions, and extremely tedious, with essentially repetitive judgments made over and over. But my father was a role model for me in his life as a civic volunteer. The way he lived that life made clear to me that he thought that this civic dimension of his life was part of his being, part of his identity. As a result, I grew up believing that civic work is integral to a life well-lived.

None of us can choose our parents, of course, and most people are not as lucky as I was. But civic guides can come in the form of teachers and mentors, as well as parents, and young people should be encouraged to find those guides. One of my favorite teachers at Phillips Exeter Academy, where I went to high school thanks to financial support from my grandmother, was an example. While I was a student there, the school principal regularly underscored to me and my classmates that the school motto, "Non Sibi"—not for self—meant that we had an obligation to be engaged in some form of civic work, vocational or avocational, for the rest of our lives. That principal, William Saltonstall, later served himself as a civic role model when he left Exeter in 1962 to head the Peace Corps in Nigeria.

My own careers in civic work were particularly shaped by three key mentors: Learned Hand, Abram Chayes, and George W. Ball. After Exeter, I went on to Harvard College and then Harvard Law School, and when I graduated from Harvard Law School, I was supremely fortunate to be chosen as law clerk for Judge Learned Hand, who shaped my civic life as much as anyone. He was among the leading American jurists of our time, and perhaps of any time. I say "perhaps" not because of any doubts of my own about his greatness, but because Hand was skeptical of superlatives, let alone hyperbole. I learned many lessons from him, but among the most valuable was the importance of craftsmanship in civic work. Careful craftsmanship is important, of course, in any work, but it is especially needed in government positions with responsibility to the public interest.

Hand was eighty-seven when I went to work for him in the Fall of 1959. He had been a federal judge for fifty years and was widely recognized as the finest legal mind in our country. Within the first week of my clerkship, I was sitting at a desk a few feet from the Judge's in the magnificent room that was his chambers at the Foley Square Courthouse in New York City. Our routine went something like this: After we had each read the briefs concerning a case, he would ask me to argue one side and he would urge opposing views. Sometimes we would then switch sides. In all events, Judge Hand would move back and forth, making arguments and countering them. His processes of thought were inextricably linked to his writing, for he wrote and rewrote eight, ten, and sometimes more drafts of an opinion.

The apparent significance of a case in the public eye was never a factor in the care with which Judge Hand examined a controversy. We spent many days, for example, considering and debating a case with these facts. A defendant in a criminal case was indicted for forging a check and also for knowingly trying to cash a forged check—these are two separate crimes—in circumstances that made it clear that the defendant could only have knowingly tried to cash the forged check if he had also forged it. He denied both of these offenses. The jury found him guilty of trying to cash a forged check but not of forging a check.

On appeal, the public defender representing the defendant argued that since the defendant was found not guilty of forging a check, his conviction for knowingly trying to cash a forged check should be reversed. It was logically impossible for him to have done the crime for which he was convicted, the public defender argued, while being innocent of forgery. Judge Hand and I knew that juries do not always behave logically. Indeed, what we assumed happened was that when the jury first started its deliberations some jurors argued for innocence and some for guilt. So the jury decided to compromise, and to find the defendant guilty of one crime, but not of the other. This would not have been a problem if the defendant had been found guilty of forging a check and not guilty of knowingly trying to cash a forged check. But the jury did the opposite. What to do? After hours of legal research, I could not find a case in point, nor was one cited by counsel on either side.

Ultimately, Judge Hand decided to uphold the verdict, its illogic notwithstanding, and in doing so, he established a precedent. In the end, he concluded, the appellate process should support a jury's decision, even when it cannot be logically defended, as long as a reasonable hypothesis can be drawn about what probably occurred in the jury deliberations. Judges were required to be logical, he concluded, but not juries.

Over the course of the nine months that I clerked for Judge Hand, I wrote no more than a few paragraphs that ever were included in his opinions. For, unlike other judges on the Court of Appeals for the Second Circuit at the time, he did not ask his law clerk to draft his opinions. So it was only the occasional comment that I wrote to the judge in a memorandum that might have found its way into his opinions. But by watching Judge Hand I learned the importance of taking special pride in the craft of civic work. He referred in one of his essays on Justice Oliver Wendell Holmes to "the Society of Jobbists," which honors "honest craft, gives good measure for its wages, and undertakes only those jobs which the members can do in proper workmanlike fashion." (Learned Hand. *The Spirit of Liberty*, 3rd ed. Knopf, 1974. 62.) In his view, this was a necessary feature of sound adjudication.

That same pride in craft should be an essential dimension of any civic position, a pride in doing the job correctly primarily for the satisfaction of doing it well as a craftsman rather than for the applause of an audience. None of us needs to be so noble as to ignore public reaction. In most civic jobs, though not in the judiciary, those in public office should take some account of public reactions. But I first learned from Judge Hand a lesson that I relearned in my other civic positions: if the approval of others is the primary fuel that motivates your work, your judgment is inevitably flawed. The "Society of Jobbists," has somewhat different standards in different dimensions of civic work, but the need for the highest order of craft is a constant.

Though I did not draft opinions for Judge Hand, I was fortunate during the year that I worked for him in that several other judges on the Second Circuit Court of Appeals asked me to do so. One of wisest was Judge Sterry Waterman from Vermont, who was also one of Judge Hand's good friends. I recall particularly a case that was of no great legal interest but affirmed the conviction of the mobster Frank Costello, nicknamed "the Prime Minister of the Underworld."

Another case I worked on for Judge Waterman involved a brand new judge on the Court, Judge Henry Friendly, who was also a friend of Judge Hand and someone whom Judge Hand "lobbied" the Eisenhower Administration to appoint. Friendly was finally chosen in 1959. By happenstance, Judge Friendly's daughter was one of my wife's closest friends, and Ellen and I joined Judge Friendly and his family a number of times for dinner during that year.

I learned a lesson, watching Judge Friendly, in how easily one's reputation in civic work can be altered. Superb craftsmanship is important, but it is sometimes not enough. Friendly came to the bench with a reputation not only as one of the smartest lawyers in the country, but also as a great expert in railroad reorganizations, an arcane field of the law. One of the first cases on which he wrote an opinion dealt with complex railroad reorganization. Friendly's lengthy opinion was an erudite masterpiece of craftsmanship. Just a few days after it was issued, however, the federal government, which was a party to the case, filed a motion to dismiss on the ground that the case should have gone directly to the U.S. Supreme Court. Friendly was acutely embarrassed when he realized that he had completely missed this point. Others had missed it too, but he was the expert in the field and not modest about his expertise, and the misstep galled him.

Judge Hand had a wonderful sense of humor, and working with him showed me that civic work could be fun as well as rewarding. He knew virtually every Gilbert and Sullivan lyric, and sang them to me frequently. He loved limericks too, the dirtier the better. I'll quote one of the cleaner ones that Hand used to show me the distinction between "broken" and "breached" in the context of our discussion of a contracts case. It also underscores the care in craft that he took to teach me the elements of style:

> There was a young lawyer named Lance
> Who contracted to buy some red ants.
> But the contract was broken
> When soon he felt pok'n
> The ants in his breached underpants.

He also loved toys, and once commandeered a toy truck that was an exhibit in a patent case and rode the little vehicle with sheer delight around the halls and to other judges' chambers, laughing all the way.

There is a saying about historians: "He who is nothing else but, is not even." Over the years, I have come to understand that the saying applies to everyone, certainly to those doing civic work. The one-dimensional person becomes, in time, ineffective even in that dimension. Hand had multiple dimensions: philosopher, raconteur, actor, as well as legal scholar, wise commentator on the human condition, and much more.

Hand believed that disinterestedness was the essential quality of a good judge, part of his devotion to craft. While that does not hold true in the same absolute terms for other aspects of civic work, the ability to examine a public policy with dispassionate objectivity is essential in all civic work even though one may have passionate views about the merits or demerits of that policy.

Hand never examined a case without reexamining all of the principles, no matter how basic, that were argued or that might be used in support of a position. He believed that the ability to withhold commitment can exist only in the true skeptic, one for whom doubt dispels all absolutes. He was supremely a skeptic, though never a cynic. A favorite quotation was that of Oliver Cromwell, spoken to his soldiers on the eve of battle: "I beseech ye in the bowels of Christ, think that ye may be wrong." That sentence, he said, should be placed on the portal of every courthouse in the country. A judge must, he believed, decide between conflicting values without imposing his own.

Hand did not accept the notion of natural moral laws governing human conduct. To him, there was no common standard to choose among basic values except the preference of individuals and the requirements of civic compromise. He did not, therefore, believe that there were any inherent principles of law except those that happen to have been accepted by a sufficient sector of society to be embodied in law.

This line of thought led Hand to be strongly critical of many judges, particularly Chief Justice Earl Warren and the liberal majority on the Supreme Court, because Hand thought they followed their personal resolutions of social conflicts in the name of justice. This was, in Hand's view, the basis for a famous crack by Oliver Wendell Homes. After walking with Holmes for some time, one of Holmes's friends said good-bye and "Do justice." Holmes response was: "Justice! My lad, that is not my job. I am here to play the game according to the rules."

Playing the game according to the rules was profoundly Hand's view of being a judge. He wrote the following words about Holmes, but they apply to himself as well. He was "a Liberal, a champion of Freedom," yet those "terms are only negative..."

> Freedom will do well enough as a catch word for those who are conscious of constraint, but once set free, their lives may prove more inane than when they were hemmed about... To most of us, who, like the defendant in *Trial by Jury*, loved this young lady today, and loved that young lady tomorrow, freedom is a curse; we slink back into our cages, however narrow, and our disciplines, however archaic. They are the defenses against the intolerable agony of facing ourselves. (Learned Hand. *The Spirit of Liberty*, 3rd ed. Knopf, 1974. 59.)

Hand, like Holmes, felt that agony deeply; he exulted in freedom and in the choices it offered. But in making those choices, he always recognized that he might be wrong.

Over the course of the half-century since I clerked for Judge Hand, I have come to disagree with many of his judicial decisions, and some of his judicial philosophy. But I continue to be committed to the belief that one should always be wary of moral absolutes, particularly in civic work. Some people, I recognize, will bridle at that statement. What about honesty, compassion, and other basic moral values, they ask. Are they not absolutes? In a sense, of course, they are. But in the sense that Judge Hand taught, and I learned, such moral precepts have real muscle only when applied, and in their application thorny problems can arise.

The realm of professional responsibility, for example, is full of moral precepts that clash in concrete cases, such as when to withhold the truth as a doctor or lawyer on behalf of a patient or client. Ultimately, choices must be made, and Hand was profoundly of the view that one must sometimes stake even one's life on a decision without the benefit that only faith can bring. But it is essential, he stressed, to keep in mind that one may be mistaken even as one acts, as act one often must. This reality was at the core of his commitment to focusing on the craft of his civic work and to trying continually to improve his craftsmanship.

ERNESTINE

My childhood was a series of bars and staffs, and between crescendos and decrescendos. I started playing the flute in elementary school, spending hours alone in an empty living room. "Look up, stand straight. That corner is your audience," I would hear my music teacher say throughout middle school. I would play the flute every day, memorizing page after page, line after line, note after note. Things changed in high school. My audience was no longer the plain white, geometric corner of my living room. Chris Rodriguez, a teacher at my high school, was one of the people who helped change things. I embarked on a public-service journey that began with music, and Mr. Rodriguez was an early supporter and an individual who embodies the ideals of an outstanding mentor.

I didn't know Mr. Rodriguez personally before founding my nonprofit VAMS. The Highly Gifted Magnet program that I was a part of in high school was held in Randolph Hall, and almost every teacher who taught in that hall was part of the Program. Mr. Rodriguez, a music teacher at the high school, but not in the Magnet program, was an exception. He was also remarkable in that he made his presence known every morning by standing outside his classroom and shouting at passing students, "Come on, get to class! It's a beautiful day!" By his lively presence, I knew about his energetic work around the school since I first arrived there. Sitting cross-legged in front of my locker, I would sometimes stay after school to finish homework. It was then that I often heard his shouts transform into song, "It's a beautiful day. Sky falls, you feel like it's a beautiful day. Don't let it get away." He was one of the few teachers who always lingered around campus until dinnertime, singing and strumming a guitar along with a group of students who wanted extra music lessons. His passion for music and helping youth rang loud and clear. Several of my friends who had taken his classes also raved about him. When I had to select a faculty advisor for VAMS, Mr. Rodriguez seemed to be the perfect fit.

One afternoon after school, I hurried into Randolph 164 seconds after the bell rang, hoping to catch Mr. Rodriguez before he began his after school lessons. He was already bent over a piano, running his fingers up and down the black and white keys. My own hands were filled with the VAMS constitution and bylaws I had drafted, still nervous about whether others would be interested in the organization, let alone join. "Visual Arts and Music for Society," I began to introduce VAMS and the vision when he interrupted, "I know, let's do it."

He quickly agreed to help, and his involvement grew over time. Mr. Rodriguez played a key role in our Halloween Spooktacular for orphans and homeless families across Los Angeles. We had contacted over a hundred shelters, found community sponsors, and invited people from all over the city to CBS Studio Center in Studio City, one of our local sponsors. Our attendee list was bursting with the colors of various organizations. The stack of volunteer nametags kept toppling over, and kept growing as we added on more supporters.

Wrinkled brown paper bags and half-crushed boxes of all sizes overflowed the small storage closet in Randolph Hall. We stared inside, wondering how we were going to move thirteen canopy tents, pounds of candy and cookies, bottles of face paint, and other Halloween mishmash from North Hollywood High School to CBS Studios. Most of us were still in high school, and we did not have drivers' licenses, let alone cars. This was the first time we had encountered a dilemma of this scale, and resorting to cabs and public transportation was all we could think of.

"Let me drive," Mr. Rodriguez chimed in during one of our meetings, completely overturning our plans. He volunteered to make multiple trips from North Hollywood High School to the studios with his small Nissan. "Do you know what you're getting into?" I questioned. He nodded. I suspected he didn't, but I gladly accepted his help.

We began early Sunday morning, the sun was barely up, and we had three hours to set up before the homeless children would start pouring in for our event. Mr. Rodriguez and our team had to make six excursions, back and forth. As Mr. Rodriguez left, I imagined him threading his way down Colfax Avenue, and merging onto a five-lane freeway without being able to see out his back window. Packing each ten-mile trip was like mastering the Internet game of Tetris—which takes both manual and mental agility—while wedged inside an auto like the Nissan Cube. We strategically wedged a T-shaped music stand placed against a box sound system, and ringed drums with bulging bags of candy. It was even more challenging than the Tetris game on my computer, as in addition to the L-s, squares, and T-s of Tetris, we had to fit in circles, hexagons, and long poles.

We managed to accomplish the task with Mr. Rodriguez's help and energy, which seemed driven by unabated passion from within. The carnival turned out to be a huge success; children and families left smiling and dancing to our tunes. When we began to clean up, despite having worked nonstop for ten hours, Mr. Rodriguez remained a dynamo. He helped us transport materials back to the closets of Randolph Hall, as if he were mastering Tetris just as well as he had earlier on.

That day, I admired Mr. Rodriguez's level of commitment. As the school year progressed, more and more students poured into the room where we held our meetings, coming from both doors, right and left, some familiar faces but many new ones. Since Mr. Rodriguez joined VAMS, membership burgeoned from just a dozen or so devoted individuals to a dedicated base of over two hundred volunteers in my high school alone, and I have come to appreciate his remarkable ability to mentor. Mr. Rodriguez was more than just a sounding board or someone who provided a fresh perspective, as many mentors do; he was able to support me yet let me fall, recognize achievements yet challenge me, and in the process gain my trust.

Gaining trust: this is perhaps the first step in mentorship, and trust was something Shaun Randolph reiterated to me when we spoke over the phone. Shaun had heard about my work and reached out to me through LinkedIn.com. He had worked as a youth director at Central City Community Outreach and mentored a group of at-risk, homeless youth at Skid Row in downtown Los Angeles.

During our conversation, I couldn't help but be reminded of Mr. Rodriguez. Shaun shared the importance of gaining the trust of individuals you work with. Shaun understood that trust is a key prerequisite to service, especially at direct-service organizations. People are not as open to assistance if they are not first reassured that you have their best interests at heart.

Two weeks before the start of his senior year at Liberty University, Shaun decided to sign on with AmeriCorps, a U.S. federal government program that encourages members to engage in direct public service. Coincidently, my co-author, Tom, was chairman of the Commission that started AmeriCorps and was for many years a member of the board of the successor organization, the Corporation for National and Community Service. Shaun joined AmeriCorps because he had discovered the stark difference between studying theories of social change and experiencing that change firsthand through service to others.

When Shaun packed his bags for Los Angeles, he expected that the experience would last just a year, after which he would return to Liberty University as a hero who proved his worth by working in "big bad Los Angeles." But things turned out quite differently. During his time in Los Angeles, Shaun received a powerful education in how children in poverty manage to survive. His job was to oversee an after-school program in downtown Los Angeles for homeless, at-risk children in the sixth through twelfth grade. What he initially viewed as a resume-boosting job—really no more than a short gig—soon became a passion, and Shaun extended his time in AmeriCorps from a single year commitment to two full years. "If you want to make a difference in the lives of youth at the Center, you need to be there through the good and the bad," Shaun confided, "You have to earn their trust."

Coming to understand the children he worked with and winning them over was far from easy. Shaun told me of an eleven-year-old girl, whom he called "Sandra" (not her real name), the self-appointed "boss" of all the youth with whom he was trying to work. Sandra strove to make

Shaun's job as difficult as possible. She, her two sisters, and two cousins in the program all stuck together and had a potent influence on the other students. In effect, they were running the entire program when Shaun arrived. Shaun knew that Sandra and her "posse" would be the key to whether his job would be easy or hard, enjoyable or frustrating, meaningful or futile. He had to win their trust.

A game he created called "Spotlight" became the means to gaining that trust. When he told the youth about Spotlight during his second week on the job, their eyes lit up: every week, a staff member would sit on a chair, and answer any question the students asked. Even though the students regularly met with the staff, they had never really gotten to know them in the past. Spotlight changed that completely.

Shaun was the first in the hot seat. Casually strolling over to the metal folding chair, Shaun braced himself. The thirty kids, all youth of color, living in missions or transitional housing in harsh parts of downtown, were known for their tough attitudes. They were ready to embarrass Shaun, or even make him break down.

"How many girlfriends have you had?" Sandra asked. The others then bombarded Shaun with questions ranging from his love interests to challenges he had struggled with and problems that most worried him. "What are you most afraid of?" "When was the last time you cried?" "How many girls have rejected you?" Shaun answered every question as truthfully as he possibly could, and at the end of each response, he reiterated one message, "It's okay to be transparent."

Shaun stressed that one thing everyone has in common is some understanding of pain. Although Shaun was never homeless, and he did not grow up in urban Los Angeles, he understood pain. "If we are honest about what we have been through, we can help each other heal," he said. Although the kids at first got some kicks by trying to embarrass Shaun, what started out as a hostile attempt to tear him down turned into respect and trust. The students were impressed by how truthfully Shaun responded when asked about topics that adults typically dismissed as inappropriate.

Sandra had recognized this as she sat in the middle of the group, and she felt threatened. "Let's all get this straight," she fired, "You've had some impressive answers, I guess. But at end of day, you just want us to like you, and then in a year you can go back to wherever you came from, right?"

Shaun couldn't answer. That was the way the AmeriCorps program worked. At a loss for what else to say, Shaun retorted, "If I had the opportunity to stay, I would." This offhand comment turned into a promise Shaun kept. He extended his stay at the center for an extra year, and still revisits the youth. When Shaun shared this and other experiences with me, I marveled at his openness. I came to realize that this is the way interactions with those you are trying to help should be.

Great mentors are open to sharing mistakes and failures, as these are often how we learn our most important lessons. Shaun was a wonderful example of this openness in dealing with the kids he mentored by becoming aware of the mistakes he had made, and not being afraid to admit them to others.

In addition to being open and establishing trust, good mentors provide a steady hand, as Patrick Lee did when working with Danny, a sixth grader through Tutoring for Community, a program sponsored by a branch of Stanford student government that I oversaw.

A breeze had just flown in the tall windows of the Penney Room, on the top floor of Stanford's Haas Center, a hub for public service on campus. There was the usual hum of a lady who always seemed to be singing outside. Patrick had just finished his weekly vocabulary lesson with Danny, a sixth grader from the low-income neighborhoods of East Palo Alto, whom he tutored. They were taking a break before moving onto math.

Patrick hastily sketched four empty squares next to what looked like an upside down J that was a bit lopsided from being drawn so quickly. "A, E, I, O, U," Danny raced through vowels, trying to guess the word Patrick had in mind for Hangman. "Yup, there's an O and an E," Patrick replied, writing the letters into the second and last square of the whiteboard.

Those small breaks during tutoring sessions, the transition between one practice sheet and another, were the best. Patrick and Danny got to play games, chat about their favorite football teams, girl problems, plans for college, and learn more and more about one another as the year progressed.

"More!" Danny exclaimed. The Hangman word was *more*.

Patrick's job was to tutor Danny. But he wanted not just to help Danny learn to read and write well and to solve basic math problems. He also sought to build a strong relationship and to act as a support system for Danny. "It's about doing more than what's asked for," Patrick told me, "Give what is needed, not just what is asked for." As Crystal O'Grady, a foster-care youth who then went on to study at Stanford, told Tom and me, "Personal attention makes a bigger impact than you can imagine. There are people who don't ask for help and are ignored." Mentors shouldn't just be there when they are asked for. They should be like the support poles for young saplings, guiding you as you grow yet giving you space as you mature.

My own best mentors have given me space, sometimes to stumble, but more important, to find my own path. When I was nineteen and a sophomore at Stanford, I had the good fortune to be offered a part-time job at a venture-capital firm in San Francisco called Alsop Louie Partners. Stewart Alsop, along with the firm's other founding partner Gilman Louie, mentored me in the processes of venture capital and entrepreneurship, which I came to see bears many similarities to the kinds of civic work I had already engaged in and wanted to continue. Those engaged in both civic work and entrepreneurship need to: identify a challenge to be met; find the right approach to meeting the challenge; develop a structure to further the approach; and design a long-term plan to ensure that the organization is viable over time. The fact that venture capital aims to make money through for-profit enterprises, while civic work aims to meet community needs, does not necessarily put them in conflict. In fact, many so-called social entrepreneurs seek a "double bottom line" to further a social cause and to make money that can be used to support that cause. In the process of gaining knowledge and skills in the venture-capital world, I strongly believe I became better able to engage in civic work, and wiser in doing so.

Silicon Valley is known for its close-knit network of millionaires and exclusive mixers. I first met Stewart Alsop at a mixer dedicated to connecting venture capital investors with entrepreneurs in the Stanford network. The event organizers had asked student-government leaders at Stanford to provide volunteers, and I was heavily involved in student government at the time. I had spent all my spare time in the student-government offices as executive director of the Student Services Division. I also had a budding interest in entrepreneurship, since I had founded VAMS in high school. Stanford's geographic location in Silicon Valley had thrown me into the backyard of some of the world's largest technology ventures such as Google, Facebook, and Twitter, and I was curious to know more about them. Although I had no particular interest in venture-capital financing, I decided on a whim to spare a few hours on a Tuesday evening to assist with the event. If anything, I thought, it seemed like a good opportunity to meet an interesting group of Stanford alumni.

It was my first time at the newly built Mackenzie Room, a large room with an 180-degree patio, high ceiling, and tall glass windows on the third floor of the Jen-Hsun Huang Engineering Center at Stanford. Jerry Yang, then CEO of Yahoo, was one of the keynote speakers at the mixer, and the room was filled with investors, entrepreneurs, and student volunteers. Tables were lined with champagne glasses and delicacies from Stanford Catering. It was luxury I had never experienced before.

Much more important, the six months following the event completely transformed my life. I emailed Stewart Alsop after the event, had my mom drive me to San Francisco so I could meet with him over sushi, and then found myself talking to other partners and employees at the firm. I eventually received an email that began, "We'd like to formalize a role for you with our firm…"

I later discovered that Stewart Alsop was the great-grandnephew of Theodore Roosevelt and that his father and uncle were American journalists and political analysts from the 1930s through the 1970s. During World War II, Stewart Alsop's father parachuted into the Périgord region of France to aid the French Resistance. He later covered domestic affairs for the *New York Herald Tribune*, while his uncle Joseph Alsop covered foreign affairs. Over time, Stewart Alsop became a wonderful mentor for me in the world of venture capital. He and the other partners at the firm helped me see its many connections to promoting social causes.

Beyond providing a support system, the best mentors realize they can always challenge their mentees to do their best. Viria Vichit-Vadakan and Kittiprapha "Job" Jivasantikarn realized this when they met Mr. U (who does not want his full name to be used) in Wiang Hang, Thailand. During their sophomore years in college, Viria and Job returned to their native country of Thailand and conducted research along the Thai-Burmese border. Their work helped enact a policy that allowed thousands of migrant workers in Thailand to use a postal money-transfer service. Mr. U was one of their mentors that summer, and he had also mentored several other youth in Thailand.

Hiking up to the small school near the orphanage, Viria and Job could see soldiers walking around and patrolling the valley in between the two mountains. They were wearing green military outfits with black boots, long rifles, and mud-riddled hats. Mines had already been planted along the border between Thailand and Burma, but these soldiers served as an extra warning to the Chan community, an ethnic minority in Burma that had fled to Thailand when their government backed down on a promise to provide freedom.

Viria and Job walked down an obscure narrow path, surrounded by rows and rows of crops paralleling the horizon, until they finally reached a small piece of land on the side of the road. There were no signs; nothing indicating that there was a school. There was just some cement and wood covered by bundles of hay to suggest a roof. It was the home of Mr. U, where he mentored dozens of youth along the Thai-Burmese border, children of the refugee migrant workers. Inside the single room, children would sit on the clay floor while Mr. U would stand beside the single blackboard and teach reading and writing. Outside, they ate lunch, below a hay roof overhang, surrounded by a small fence so younger kids wouldn't wander too far. "It was a simple accommodation," Viria shared, "But it was so much better than having them around the fields."

It was another dry, hot sunny day and pesticides once again rained down on the crops like a light drizzle. But the oranges and bugs were not the only ones touched by the toxins—so were children working in the fields. Sweat mixed with chemicals, and the children frequently complained about headaches. Mr. U had negotiated with owners of the orange plantations to allow that school nearby, and he also decided to set up his daycare center to provide an escape for the children. But beyond that, he wanted to educate them: teach them Thai and enable them to interact with people outside the refugee community. "Without school, they wouldn't have a chance to be educated," Mr. U shared. "They would just remain in the fields with their health deteriorating as they grow up." Mr. U wanted to challenge the kids to learn, no matter how old they were. "He was persistent. Working on this issue is sometimes frustrating. You can't really do anything," Job said, "But Mr. U sees future in these kids. He tries to challenge them to see it too and fix a fundamental problem."

Mentors have also helped me realize the importance of challenging both my traditional beliefs and myself. Upon joining Alsop Louie Partners, I found that I really enjoyed interacting with entrepreneurs, and I identified my first investment for the firm within two months of starting work at the firm. By then, I was already co-authoring this book on civic engagement with Tom, another important mentor in my life. Working with both Tom and partners at the firm enabled me to be better able to promote civic work on the one hand and venture capital on the other, and in the process balance both the for-profit and the nonprofit world.

I do not suggest that all venture capitalists have the best of social intentions. But I have found that many of my role models in the venture-capital world are extraordinarily philanthropic in terms of both their money and their time, apart from their vocational work. Brook Byers, for example, is one of the founders of Kleiner Perkins Caufield and Byers, one of the largest venture-capital firms in Silicon Valley, and was instrumental in forming the Byers Eye Institute at Stanford Hospital and Clinics, which is dedicated to combating blindness. Bill Coleman has been a founder and leader in many Silicon Valley startup companies and also founded the Coleman Institute for Cognitive Disabilities at the University of Colorado. Gilman Louie, one of the founders of Alsop Louie Partners, engages in an interesting mix of civic work and venture-capital advising. He frequently travels from Silicon Valley to Washington, D.C. to advise the United States intelligence agencies, and he serves on a congressional commission and a number of government advisory boards.

Another extraordinary example of a leader who is both a successful venture investor and philanthropist is Bill Draper. He began his career as a traditional venture capitalist, working in his father's firm. In 1965, he founded Sutter Hill Ventures, one of the leading venture-capital firms in Silicon Valley today. He later took a break from venture capital to work in government, serving as president and chairman of the Export-Import Bank of the United States, and as CEO of the United Nations Development Program. He currently serves as general partner of Draper Richards LP, a venture-capital fund focused on early-stage technology companies in the U.S., as well as co-chair of the Draper Richards Kaplan Foundation, a venture philanthropy fund focused on start-up nonprofit organizations promoting social change around the world. He also cares deeply about ensuring that future generations will be involved in both realms, as he made clear when he spoke at an entrepreneurship course I started at Stanford, as I later discuss in Lesson 7.

Moreover, as my mentors have helped me understand, venture capital has the potential to address critical sectors in our nation that require social innovation — energy, education, and medicine, to name just three. With the right intentions, I believe venture capital can be deployed in ways that fund disruptive ideas and further civic benefits for our country and the world. Gilman Louie realized this during his time leading the CIA's venture-capital arm, In-Q-Tel. As the first CEO of In-Q-Tel, he had an explicit objective to enhance national security by connecting the federal government's intelligence community with promising new technologies and entrepreneurial startups in the private sector. One successful investment that Gilman supported was Keyhole, a satellite mapping software, with sophisticated 3D imagery, now known as Google Earth. United States military and security agencies used Keyhole during the first Iraq War in 2003.

Other individuals who have worked at Alsop Louie Partners and have also been involved in government service include three former partners at In-Q-Tel, and a former deputy director of the National Security Agency, Bill Crowell. These individuals have all served as helpful mentors during my journey in venture capital, demonstrated interest in my own civic work, and shaped my attitudes towards government and civic work. Gilman has often challenged me with the following question: What role can venture capital have in shaping the future in ways that will directly benefit our shrinking planet and its peoples? How can venture capital help ensure that the next 25 years will be as productive as the last 25 years?

Finally, one of my most important mentors has been my co-author, Tom. Although separated by almost six decades in age, and despite generational differences, Tom has been an important influence in my life. I first met him near the beginning of my sophomore year at Stanford, when the executive director of Stanford's Center on Philanthropy and Civil Society, Kim Meredith, introduced us to one another. I had never met a senior university administrator, much less someone who served in so many other capacities as Tom has done. I would have been enthusiastic and humbled to have Tom as a supporter. But that wasn't enough for him. Tom asked that I co-author this book with him, and since then, he has become not only a mentor and teacher, but also a collaborator and friend.

Tom's ability to serve in these various roles is illustrated by the times we worked together holding focus-group interviews to hear from other youth engaged in civic work. Old Union is a place where Stanford students often converge to play air hockey, watch football on one of two large plasma televisions, or grab a snack at The Axe and Palm Café. My favorite room is one with plush tan sofas that form a messy circle along the walls. One wall is covered in long clear glass panels, so that I can always see a few wayfarers walking by. Tom and I met with dozens of students over the course of several evenings. Some were undergraduates at Stanford, while others came from elsewhere. During our first session, I noticed a few more bypassing observers than usual, staring and perhaps questioning the unusual arrangement. A couple students sat cross-legged on the floor. Others hugged their knees on the sofa. And one man almost four times my age, with just as much energy, sat side by side with the students, listening to their stories. Tom wasn't afraid to venture out of his office to listen to and support other young people.

Tom is one among many role models, mentors, and teachers who have guided me in my civic journey and pushed me further than I ever thought I could have gone. I was initially a bewildered young student, looking for help, and what success I have had can be attributed to good mentors who have lent their hands. Some are engaged in civic work as a vocation, some as an avocation, and some have moved back and forth from the public sector to the private sector while remaining constant in their commitment to that work. I am enormously grateful for the support of those mentors. Early on in my career, they have inspired me while challenging me, and challenged me while supporting me. But I also realize that doors will not often open unless you knock on them and push a little. Good mentors exist, but you need to be proactive in seeking their help. Once found, their value is immeasurable.

LESSON 2

Civic Work Should Serve the Public Interest

TOM AND ERNESTINE

It may at first seem obvious that civic work should serve the public interest, but we have found that thinking through what is the public interest and how best to serve that interest can be challenging issues. We explain this critical concept through multiple examples drawn from our own experiences and the experiences of a number of young people who are engaged in civic work. From these stories emerge our judgment that serving the public interest means a primary focus on helping to promote the common good as opposed to individual gain. We do not believe that pure altruism must be the sole reason for civic work. This is rarely the case, as we discuss motives to engage in civic work in Lesson 4. But we do believe that a sense of social responsibility as the basis for civic work is what differentiates it from activities that may assist others, but are primarily based on personal gain.

As the pages that follow make clear, civic work may take many different forms. For Tom, government service and politics has been the primary form, as his section recounts, though he has been active in many nonprofit organizations helping the public interest as well. In such challenging times as the Cuban Missile Crisis, those with whom Tom worked on that seminal event struggled with what actions would be in the public interest. He was conflicted personally when called to help represent the United States Government in the Supreme Court when he thought its legal position was erroneous, though he did so because he thought it was in the public interest to ensure that the Government's position had a fair hearing.

For Ernestine, and for most of the young civic volunteers whom we interviewed, promoting public policies or partisan politics was not the primary focus of their civic work, as her section makes clear. Her stories reflect many other aspects of serving the public interest such as providing basic human needs through nonprofit organizations, as is the passion of one young person she highlights, and fighting human trafficking, as is the civic work of another. As we spoke to these young women and men, we heard striking tales of extraordinary dedication to helping others through a wide range of civic organizations, some domestic and some international. As these stories make clear, we view the public interest as a broad umbrella under which a range of civic activities can occur.

TOM

Abram Chayes was my teacher at Harvard Law School and was an active supporter of John F. Kennedy in his campaign for the presidency. When Kennedy won, Chayes gained an appointment as Legal Adviser in the State Department, the position he sought, though he had no experience in international law. I had the great good fortune to come to work for Chayes in Washington in 1962. Chayes was a particularly good civic mentor for me after Judge Hand. Chayes was an activist and would never have been comfortable as a judge whose professional responsibility was to react to the claims of adversaries. Chayes wanted to create law in the furtherance of social justice, while Hand was deeply skeptical of those with that mindset. But both of them were committed to the notion that their roles were to serve the public and its interest as best as they were able.

Over the years, I have found myself much closer to Chayes in my views of law, including the roles of law in serving society. Chayes opened my mind to think more broadly and deeply than I had before about how civic work can serve the public interest. As one example, I have come to view Chief Justice Earl Warren as the most significant

American judge in my lifetime, a view that Chayes would have shared, while Hand disparaged him because Hand thought Warren's intellect was weak. Hand believed that Warren was too prone to use his position to further his judgments of what was socially sound for society. Although Warren was not an intellectual giant, as was Hand, Warren was able to use his position to reshape American society in terms of civil rights and liberties, most famously in fashioning a unanimous opinion striking down school segregation in *Brown v. Board of Education, 347 U.S. 483 (1954).*

Although Chayes shifted from Cambridge to Washington and from professor to government official, he was still a teacher and I remained his student when I joined him as his special assistant. I reported for work on what became known as "Cuba Monday," October 22, 1962. Soviet-built missiles with nuclear-strike capability had been discovered in Cuba, and that night President Kennedy announced that United States warships would impose "a strict quarantine" that would block "all offensive military equipment under shipment to Cuba." From 8:00 p.m. to 8:00 a.m. the following morning, I worked with Chayes and another colleague on a memorandum explaining the legal basis for the Unites States' action. Although, like Chayes, I had never taken a course in international law, we quickly steeped ourselves in the legal rules that applied to nations in times of peace and in times of war. After a tense week in which nuclear war seemed—and actually was—a real possibility, the Soviet Union backed down and agreed to withdraw its missiles from Cuba. Since the story of what has come to be termed "The Cuban Missile Crisis" has been told often and at length, there is no need for me to repeat it here. But I will use it as an example of the way in which "the public interest" was ultimately judged by a wise president and shaped in legal terms by a resourceful legal adviser. The case also illustrates that an effective lawyer in government will not simply defend the public policies made by other officials, but will also be directly engaged in helping to decide those policies.

A key initial step in the Cuban Missile Crisis was to refer publically at all times to the U.S. action as a "quarantine" rather than a "blockade," because a "blockade" is an act of war under international law, and the President and his advisers wanted to minimize the Russian claim that the United States was engaged in an act of war while effectively preventing further Soviet missiles from reaching Cuba. The "quarantine" label was first suggested by the Deputy Legal Adviser, Leonard Meeker, who was in the key initial White House meetings because Chayes was away, although Chayes returned immediately to Washington just before the President's public announcement of the quarantine. Labeling the U.S. action a "quarantine" rather than a "blockade," might seem just a bit of legalese, but it was actually a key to the developing United States policy, which was to stop further Soviet shipments of missiles while avoiding acts of war under international law. The designation "quarantine" and the legal case that we prepared to defend the U.S. action were central to our ultimate success in persuading the overwhelming majority of countries within the United Nations to reject the Soviet position and support the United States.

Some leading U.S. foreign policy experts, including former Secretary of State Dean Acheson, urged the president not to worry about international law, but rather to bomb the missile bases in Cuba without delay. If a legal argument was needed, he and other advisors argued, the United States should simply claim it was acting in self-defense. The United Nations Charter is clear in stating that its terms do not limit "the inherent right of individual or collective self-defense if an armed attack occurs…" Acheson and those supporting his position claimed it was a legal technicality that no actual "armed attack" had occurred because it might occur at any time. Fortunately, wiser judgments prevailed, initially led by then Attorney General Robert F. Kennedy, who saw that the issues at stake involved how our government would best represent that it was defending not just the American "public interest," but the public interest of the free world.

The legal case we made was rooted in an action by the Organization of American States (OAS), which included twenty countries, and from which Cuba had been excluded. A key OAS treaty (the so-called "Rio Treaty") provided that the OAS members were obligated to provide assistance to any American State "to meet armed attacks against" that State and "to deal with threats of aggression against any of them." Secretary of State Rusk himself presented the United States position that the secret build-up of nuclear missiles in Cuba constituted a "threat of aggression" within the meaning of the Rio Treaty and, therefore, triggered a necessary response in support of the quarantine.

In this process, we had to keep constantly in mind how best to express the public interest, not just in terms of defending the quarantine of Cuba, but in the longer-run as well. We concluded that promoting a policy that would help ensure that the United States would act in collaboration with regional allies would both strengthen the persuasiveness of United States actions to other nations outside the region, and would also temper the likelihood that the United States would act unilaterally with military force in subsequent situations when there might be domestic pressures to do so.

History has shown that we were much more successful in the first of those aims than in the second. Adlai Stevenson, as the United States Ambassador to the United Nations, made a dramatic showing of the extent to which Russian missiles were actually on the ground in Cuba and could quickly be used to attack America. But it was no less important that the arguments of the Soviet Union in the UN be effectively countered. Those arguments were made in essentially legal terms. The Soviets claimed that the quarantine—which they labeled a "blockade"—was in violation of the United Nations Charter and generally recognized principles of international law.

The United States was able to make a compelling two-part legal case in response to the Soviet arguments. The first part was that the United States was faced with "a threat of aggression" within the meaning of the Rio Treaty, and the governing body of the Rio Treaty voted 18 to 0 to support the U.S. position. The second part was that the United Nations Charter expressly provides that "nothing in the present Charter precludes the existence of regional arrangements or agencies for dealing with such matters relating to the maintenance of international peace and security as are appropriate for regional action" provided they are consistent with "the "purposes and Principles of the United Nations." Our carefully crafted legal case made clear that the Rio Treaty established just the type of "regional arrangement" referred to in the UN Charter, and that the quarantine, supported by that regional arrangement, was consistent with the UN's "Purposes and Principles." Over the course of the next few days leading up to the Soviet agreement to withdraw its missiles, this legal case was viewed as compelling to most UN members, in significant part because the United States was not simply engaged in armed intervention on its own, but rather was joined in a multinational effort to head off what might quickly become World War III.

With the successful conclusion of the Cuban Missile Crisis, I thought it likely those U.S. policy makers would see the public-policy advantages of multinational actions and that unilateral military interventions by the United States would be a thing of the past. Unfortunately, I was wrong. The U.S. invaded the Dominican Republic on the thinnest possible legal basis in 1965, and the Vietnam War quickly escalated after that with much more tragic consequences.

Meanwhile, for much of the next six months after the Cuban Missile Crisis, I spent considerable time on various legal aspects of our policy toward Cuba, including our increased efforts to isolate that country from interactions with the U.S. and other Western countries. In retrospect, I think this policy was a profound mistake. We would, I believe, be in far better shape in terms of our military position as well as our leadership in the Americas if we had sought to strengthen economic and political ties with Cuba from the time of the revolution led by Fidel Castro. But, of course, I was not making the key policy judgments at the time.

While working for Chayes, I had other opportunities to help consider how best to further "the public interest" while serving as a lawyer representing the United States. For example, I traveled to Panama to help defend before an international tribunal the U.S. actions in the wake of riots in the Canal Zone. I also assisted Chayes in an arbitration with France that was held in Geneva and involved international aviation rights. These were the kinds of fascinating problems that I was able to work on, and I enjoyed the experiences enormously. Many of these issues not only gave me rich insights into the varieties of issues involved in serving "the public interest" as a U.S. government lawyer, they also provided raw materials for the first books that I wrote, one of which I co-authored with Chayes and one of his other assistants, Andreas Lowenfeld, who became a distinguished professor at New York University School of Law. Our three-volume work, titled "International Legal Process," involved an entirely different approach to teaching international law than had ever been followed, using actual problems facing international policy makers to teach the knowledge and skills needed in practicing public international law.

Lawyers in private practice must have clients, but government lawyers, charged with representing "the public interest," face an interesting issue when asked to name their clients. As the senior lawyer in the State

Department, in one sense Chayes worked for the Secretary of State, Dean Rusk. But on many issues such as the Cuban Missile Crisis, Chayes was working directly with the president and his chief National Security advisers in the White House. His work often did not include anyone else who was designated a legal adviser. The White House counsel was primarily lawyer for the president on personal matters. It is only under the aegis of Vice President Dick Cheney that either the president or vice president has thought he could or should have his own lawyer on legal issues of national security.

Chayes taught me that while he "worked for" the Secretary of State, the American people were his client, and that civic work requires a degree of independence of judgment that should not be overruled even by the Secretary of State. As he stressed to me, we had to keep in mind that our civic work must serve the public interest. In theory, Secretary Rusk might have fired Chayes if their judgments had clashed too sharply. But this course would have had its own set of risks, particularly if Chayes had chosen to air publicly whatever caused the rift. In fact, Rusk—who started law school but never finished his legal education—had great respect for Chayes, a view that was reinforced by the Deputy Secretary of State George W. Ball, who was himself a renowned international lawyer with many years of experience in the field.

Like Chayes, I think the public is the sole "client" of every government official. In the case of a city employee, the public is the citizens of the city. In the case of the federal government, it is all Americans. Every federal official takes an oath to "support and defend the Constitution of the United States...." It might seem that there is always a court somewhere to determine whether a federal official is really carrying out his or her duties under the Constitution and U.S. laws. But, as I learned first-hand when working in the State Department, many, and probably most, issues about whether a government official is obeying the law can never be adjudicated by a court because no one has "standing," which means the right to sue.

As a young government lawyer at the end of 1962, for example, I decided which State Department documents concerning Lee Harvey Oswald and other matters would be sent to the Warren Commission appointed by President Johnson to investigate the assassination of President Kennedy. For weeks immediately after the terrible day that Kennedy was shot, I poured over every document that I could find relating

to Oswald. Since he had spent time in Cuba and was married to a
Russian, rumors were swirling around that a Communist conspiracy was
involved and that Oswald was simply a pawn. In the end, the Warren
Commission concluded that Oswald acted on his own, though books
appear almost every year to dispute that judgment. This was just one of
the extraordinarily interesting assignments that I had, though I was not
yet thirty years old. My point here, however, is that I was given major
responsibility as part of the investigation, but no one could sue on the
ground that I should have flagged and sent to the Commission some
item that I omitted. As part of my responsibility, I had extraordinary
opportunities in the State Department to help consider what were
sound "public policies," and then to implement those policies.

In a few situations, however, I was called on to represent the United
States Government even when I thought its policies were completely
wrong. One that comes particularly to mind involved a case before the
United State Supreme Court, *Herbert Aptheker, et al v. The Secretary
of State*, 378 U.S. 500 (1964). Mr. Aptheker was a U.S. citizen who had
been denied a U.S. passport because he was a member of a Communist
organization and under the terms of the Subversive Activities Control
Act, he was prohibited from applying for a U.S. passport, without which
he could not travel abroad. Aptheker claimed that he had a constitu-
tional right to travel abroad, a right that could not be abridged by U.S.
officials who were implementing an act of Congress. The Justice Department turned to Chayes and me to represent the United States in
defending the Congressional statute. We both personally thought that
Subversive Activities Control Act was unconstitutional in authorizing
the denial of a U.S. passport to Aptheker, but we also thought that the
case, since it arose under a statute that was approved by Congress and
signed by President Truman, should be adjudicated by the Supreme
Court with the lawyers for the U.S. Government making the best possible arguments for the statute's validity. On this basis, Chayes and I
fashioned the strongest legal arguments we could, while personally hoping that the Supreme Court would decide for Aptheker, as it did, by a
vote of 6 to 3. We felt that we had properly defended the "public
interest," and that the Supreme Court rightly decided that interest. In
2011, the Obama Administration took a different view when it decided
not to defend the Defense of Marriage Act against a claim of unconsti-

tutionality, one of the few times, insofar as I know, when an administration has reached such a judgment regarding an act of Congress.

ERNESTINE

I remember my first political election. I was sitting in a corner of my fourth-grade classroom where all the tables nicely converged, and everyone was passing sheets of paper to their right and left, until they all eventually landed in a giant pile in front of me. A few students, myself included, tried to read through the turned-over ballots, attempting to glimpse what others had penciled in on the back of the thin sheets of paper. I mostly saw backward G's and occasionally B's.

It was the 2000 Bush-Gore election. "Class, today is an important day. Election Day. We'll be voting in class," the teacher had announced, and then proceeded to spell out rules and regulations. We each got a sheet of paper about the size of my hand. "This is your ballot," she said, "You have the right to receive a new ballot if, prior to casting your ballot, you believe you made a mistake." She asked us what we knew about the three candidates on the ballot—Bush, Gore, and Nader—but only a few students seemed to know anything about the candidate's views.

Having that empty ballot in front of me for ten minutes was a bit nerve-wracking. I wasn't very knowledgeable about current events and politics at the time. I remember hearing adults talk about one candidate advocating for personal retirement accounts using Social Security money, and another arguing that the budget surplus should be used to strengthen Medicare. But I was barely old enough to claim double digits in my age, and Medicare was the last thing on my mind.

So I voted for Nader, not because I supported his platform—I knew little about what he favored—but because no one else in my class seemed to like him. I wasn't really sure how politics worked. I was far from voting age, but being able to pencil in a candidate's names and pretend that I had a judgment that should be counted was surreal. I might well have remained in this state of ignorance except for another political experience in high school.

Five years after my first "vote," I found myself at the Democratic Office in San Fernando Valley, toying with the coiled cord of an outdated telephone on a cheap plastic table, in an office next to a 99 cents store on one side and a discount clothing store on the other. It was another 90-degree day in Los Angeles, and I had escaped into the air-conditioned office to make a series of telephone calls. I wasn't sure what was easier, making phone call after phone call in a small, stuffy office or walking from door-to-door in the sweltering heat. We had a list of people who had aligned themselves with the Democratic Party but hadn't voted in the past few years. Our charge was to convert their apathy into action. Making phone calls was like a race to see who could punch in numbers, balance a pen and phone in one hand, and convert the most number of people in the shortest amount of time. Walking and passing out flyers was like seeing who could operate a factory in the heat: we had a small assembly line for the flyers, where one person would rip off a piece of masking tape and roll it up into a small double-sided adhesive, while another person would dab the tape on the back of the flyer, and then a third person would whack the flyer on the wall of a building or house. These activities were demanding, a combination of sprints and a marathon.

Kailim Toy, my AP United States history teacher, had scurried us out of the classroom and asked us each to perform at least ten hours of political volunteering after we had studied a good deal about how politics had affected American history since the founding of the country. My fellow classmates and I were not old enough to vote, but we devoted our time to political parties, either the Democrats or the Republicans, depending on our choice, ballot propositions advocating for a tobacco tax, and local district elections, activities that were all designed to serve the public interest. From that experience, I was able to gain a better understanding of the importance of political processes. Mr. Toy encouraged us all to continue engaging in these and other political activities that moved beyond academics and directly served the public interest.

Serving the "public interest" can take many different forms of civic work that do not include politics or the kinds of government service in which Tom was engaged for much of his career. Some of the young civic volunteers whom Tom and I interviewed were involved in promoting public policies or in partisan politics, but many more were not. As we spoke to these young women and men, we heard striking stories of extraordinary dedication to helping others through a wide range of civic organizations, some domestic and some international. When we asked their views about partisan politics, many said that they thought their time, energy, and efforts would better serve the public interest by civic work with a nonprofit group that directly helped people or communities in need. This type of civic work, they said, gave them more satisfaction and sense of personal fulfillment, a feeling of being part of something larger than themselves. When we pressed a bit, some suggested that politics frequently seemed too influenced by money and that politicians often appeared so beholden to major donors that politics had less appeal than direct work for these nonprofit groups, though they well understood the importance of direct participation in politics to help make democracy work.

My own story and the stories of some of my friends engaged in helping this kind of civic organization may explain why I believe passionately that assisting people in need can serve the general welfare of the public—and therefore be in the public interest—as opposed to particular and private interests. As these stories make clear, I view the public interest as a broad umbrella under which a range of civic activities can occur.

Luis Ortiz was one individual with whom Tom and I spoke. I have helped Luis recruit volunteers for the Latin American nonprofit organization Un Techo para mi País ("A Roof for My Country"). In working with Luis, I learned how constructing transitional houses for people who literally had no roof over their heads serves the "public interest." As Luis explained their plight, this civic organization provides a basic human necessity—a home—to those who cannot afford to buy or construct their own. In time, those people may gain the resources to acquire their own houses, but in the interim, this group ensures that they will have a place to call "home."

I remember when Luis told me about one day when he splashed his face over and over again, allowing warm water to trickle down the crevices of his grimy forehead and cheeks. He rubbed his bloodshot eyes and the ridge of his nose, with water splashing across his shoulders as he did so. But he still felt dirty. He had just returned from "The Ice," a small village in central Mexico City that was aptly named for its cold weather. Luis recalled frigid wind rushing past his bare skin when he visited a makeshift bathroom, located in the middle of the stalks of corn. There was no toilet, let alone any sewage system in the community.

Beyond the cold, Luis recalled the grim life of the residents, living in mud. He remembered kids with their knees covered with mounds of dried dirt, attempting to push wooden toy cars across the mud. The mud pushed back at the wheels of their cars, preventing them from moving any distance except ever so slowly and gradually.

Luis lived in "The Ice" for three days, during which he worked with Un Techo para mi País, lifting planks of wood, hammering nails, and ultimately building a home. The best part of his trip was when he finished building the home. It remained clean for a few minutes until one of the boys ran inside the house, and pushed his soiled car across the clean wooden floor planks. The toy rolled smoothly, quicker than it even had before, leaving a thick streak of dirt in its trail as it traveled. That was one moment that confirmed Luis' interest in serving the public, particularly in helping those in need of the basic necessities of life. Although he had felt filthy on the outside, he felt clean and pure on the inside. And, upon returning home, taking that lukewarm shower wasn't enough. His work wasn't over. He knew he could feel cleaner both inside and out. He had to do more than help that one family. He had to build more houses.

For Kevin Mo and Muthu Alagappan, serving the public interest was about providing access to health care to those who were most at risk. They volunteered at the South Asian Preventive Health Outreach Program (SAPHOP) at Stanford. One project they organized through SAPHOP was a preventive health intervention for taxi drivers at San Francisco International Airport and Mineta San José International Airport. The program consisted of health screenings, dietary recommendations, and free exercise materials to prevent or mitigate heart disease for taxi drivers who regularly consumed fast food.

Kevin and Muthu told us about a time when they were with a group of college students outside Terminal 5 of the airport in San Jose. Some simple medical equipment was scattered on two tables. "What did you eat for breakfast?" Kevin asked, as he proceeded to walk with one taxi driver through a health screening. "Double-double hamburger," the taxi driver chuckled. "What's with all you youngsters coming down here with medical equipment pretending you're doctors? Us taxi drivers always get stuck on the bottom rung," Kevin's patient continued. "We always get the worst; they don't even bring us real doctors."

Kevin instructed the taxi driver to place his palms on two metal handles attached to a screen. The metal sensor was designed to calculate one's heart rate, though it looked more like a Game Boy with two protruding ends. As the screen flashed 142—high blood pressure—the taxi driver was getting visibly angry.

"You think you know what you're doing, but you don't!" Negative comments like this continued for three hours as Kevin screened over a hundred taxi drivers with his friend Muthu and other students. It was a Saturday, and the airport was bustling with drivers coming in and out. The students had just finished testing a wave of drivers and were getting ready to pack up. Three cars, trunks opened wide, were lined up side by side on the sidewalk.

Muthu began lifting blood pressure pumps, calculators, and heart-rate monitors into his car when a yellow cab pulled into the terminal. This driver seemed a bit more hurried than others. A Middle Eastern man, wearing a polo shirt with a few grease stains, yanked the door open. He had just finished his shift. With his eyes focused on the medical students, he walked briskly over to them.

"Can I be screened?" he asked. Muthu paused for a second. "Sure." Muthu and Kevin could have just left that day. Neither had signed up to volunteer for more than three hours. But they decided to put aside other commitments, to unpack all their supplies, and to walk the man through a health screening. As Muthu told me, "When your mission is to provide health outreach, every single person matters." "If someone needs screening, we must do it," Kevin concurred.

Despite the gripes they had received during the day, Kevin, Muthu, and the other student volunteers realized that serving the public interest could mean providing individuals access to health care. It is about taking the extra step because it will help someone in need.

For me, serving the public interest has included visiting senior centers and sharing the power of music. One of my first visits to a senior center in Los Angeles was confusing, to say the least. I really didn't know how to entertain a group of much older people. But at the end of my visit, I felt that I better understood the importance and power of civic work.

I entered a side door of the center near a collection of garbage bins, and began walking past identically furnished rooms, each with a couple of beds, two chairs, and a single window. In one room, I saw an elderly

Caucasian woman sitting on the edge of a light blue bed. Thick creases defined her eyelids, and bags lined the bottom of her beady eyes. She stared at me, and her wrinkled, weathered hand moved back and forth, while her face showed no expression.

"Why is she sad?" I thought, wondering if she had heard I was there to perform. I passed by patients in other rooms before finally entering one at the end of the hallway. The patient in this room was lying flat on a gurney, although the sheet covering her legs rippled slightly, seeming to suggest that she was trying to escape from me as I entered with a nurse. Her head turned away from the door as I came in to her hospital room. I felt a shove from behind. Another nurse was weaving through the door of the room, where I had been standing. His energy starkly contrasted that of the women on the bed. Yanking the blinds open, he cried, "You have visitors!" and light flooded into the room.

I saw the woman's eyelids pinch shut. The nurse tugged a switch near the bed, tilting the head of the gurney upward and toward me. But the woman kept trying to shift even further away from where I was standing.

I didn't know what to do. Finally, I tiptoed next to her and gently laid a sugar cookie and card printed with happy faces near the blood-pressure monitor on her nightstand, and then left. I departed as quickly as I had arrived, and fortunately, it was almost time for me to start my music performance.

With a flute case in one hand, music stand in another, and several loose sheets of music and homemade greeting cards almost spilling from my purse, I passed other elderly people—many of whom also seemed detached and listless—and entered their recreation room. It was a plain room with only board games and bingo cards brightening the coffee tables. A handful of seniors were already there, talking and playing cards.

I began assembling my flute, arranging sheets of music, and shortening the height of my stand so that I could see across it, though barely. Meanwhile, other seniors shuffled into the room, including the beady-eyed lady whom I had encountered earlier. As they settled themselves in the front rows, other men and women on gurneys were rolled into the back and arranged like lopsided sentinels. One woman had plastic tubes protruding from her arms. She was in even worse shape than the woman I had encountered earlier, and her presence added to my already heightened fear.

Nervously, I picked up my flute and began. As I played, my eyes occasionally moved from the black and white notes on the staff to the audience. I met the unexpected glassy gaze of an elderly man, trembled, and stumbled upon a note. I had been playing for about thirty minutes when a few sheets of my music fluttered to the floor. I looked away, played a few more notes, and decided to end the recital.

"Did they like it?" I worried as I packed my bag. I wondered if the beady-eyed lady who had seemed so listless and sad enjoyed my performance. This question remained in my head when I felt someone approach me from behind.

Turning, I found myself inches away from an almost perfectly circular pair of eyes, a wrinkled face—hers. Then her clammy hand gently squeezed mine, and a smile emerged in her crinkled eyes. Over time, small gestures like these have reassured me that civic work should simply serve the public interest. I realized that day the rewards of civic work are not always evident. The people you reach out to sometimes do not welcome your help. Your rewards are often not perceptible, let alone visible. The chances of being thanked for your work are often minimal, and seeing a smile on the face of someone you help can be the best expression of gratitude.

Racquel Enad encountered similar challenges when she interned at Visayan Forum Foundation during the summer after her freshman year of college. Racquel had come to the Philippines to assist those who had been the subjects of human trafficking, or modern-day slavery.

Racquel's sister Kat had been volunteering at Visayan Forum for the past three months, and she warned Racquel, "Change happens slowly here. It'll be a struggle." But just thinking about her job description, Racquel thought she knew exactly what she was going to do and eagerly anticipated the work in Cebu. Talking to individuals at Visayan Forum seemed more than feasible, especially with her educational background in global health and her research interests in human trafficking. Her self-assurance and commitment was strengthened upon arriving at the anti-human trafficking organization and meeting the co-regional director. Ligaya was a small yet dynamic Filipino woman. Her fiery attitude and contagious enthusiasm made Racquel ever more excited to work for the organization. She recalled her sister's warnings and wondered whether they were really accurate. Lying in bed that night, glancing at the open sky sprinkled with a few stars, she felt at ease and comfortable, despite the adjustment usually needed for a new environment.

The next day, Racquel approached a group of Filipino domestic workers, or "maids" who had been mistreated by their employers. Many of them were teenage girls, who were working fifteen-hour plus days to clean, cook, and care for their employers' families. Some were even suffering abuses beyond having to work long hours. Visayan Forum sought to provide them comprehensive support and advocacy. Standing amongst the group of strangers, Racquel slowly gazed around her, momentarily pausing to examine each woman before her.

A young boy scuttled up to the Filipino women, chattering and joking, with mannerisms that made it obvious he was referring to Racquel. "Hush!" one of the women scolded. "You know she can understand?" Everyone, except Racquel, chortled.

It was at that moment that Racquel realized that she could not help the women in the way she wanted to. She felt a sense of confusion, a perplexity that was not like the reaction she felt in her years of academic classes. The women were not comfortable sharing their experiences with her. The perfect little paragraph describing her job was no longer relevant.

"I don't know why I came," Racquel sobbed to her sister, "What am I going to do now? This is all just a huge mistake."

"Stick around and follow me with my work," her sister Kat responded. "You do have a purpose here." Racquel reluctantly agreed, and over the next few days and weeks, the situation did improve. She still felt discouraged, however, by the seemingly slow progress. Meetings with directors were constantly rescheduled and emergencies always mysteriously arose. "Corruption, self-interest, and bureaucracy hindered my efforts," Racquel told me.

As her summer experience was coming to an end, Racquel finally decided to bring up these problems at a meeting with Ligaya. The meeting was supposed to begin at 2:00 p.m. She was just about to leave her house when Ligaya sent her a text message, requesting to meet thirty minutes later. This wasn't a problem for Racquel, as seemingly every single meeting during her stay in the Philippines was rescheduled. Racquel did not even feel guilty when at 2:30 p.m., she was stuck in traffic, and she had to ask Ligaya to push the meeting back even further. Finally, an hour after the scheduled time, Ligaya and Racquel were able to meet in a café. Troubled and frustrated, Racquel blurted out to Ligaya, "How do you do it? How do you keep working in this field, when it seems that every time you take a step forward, you get pushed back ten steps?"

Without hesitation, Ligaya replied, "My life motto, Racquel, is 'to spread goodness.' I may not change the system, but if I can spread goodness to at least one person, and that person spreads goodness to another, I know I have done my job. That is how I keep going, and that is how I go to bed at night."

These powerful words of advice, to spread goodness to at least one person, became Racquel's focus for the rest of her time in the Philippines and beyond. As my friend Michael Tubbs, who founded a nonprofit called The Phoenix Scholars and ran for Stockton City Council, told me, "It's about the power of one. If you change the life of one child, you can change one family, one block, one community." Serving the public interest can mean making a difference now in the world by making a difference in just one person's life.

There are many ways to serve the public interest. You can engage in politics and government work, as Tom discussed, or volunteer for the kinds of civic organizations that I have been describing. You can help build homes for those in need, provide access to health care, or serve your local community in other ways to improve conditions for those in need. I have learned that often those we are trying to help do not thank us, and we need to remember that the sense of accomplishment in assisting others is its own reward. Sometimes, of course, we do receive expressions of gratitude, and one such experience at the Golden Acres Senior Center will always be vivid in my memory.

The day was finally winding down, and I was making my last run around Golden Acres Senior Center, gathering all the materials my VAMS colleagues and I had scattered around their activities room. Bingo cards, check. Pens, check. Amidst the hustle, I felt a slight tap on the shoulder. "Beautiful child, take this." A slender, white-haired woman with fine crinkles near her eyes placed a piece of paper in my hand, gently pushing it towards me even after I grasped it by the edge. It was the paper we had used to tally scores for the Valentine's Day Bingo Tournament, just minutes ago. I unfolded the note, penned half cursive, half print:

To our beloved student visitors,

Belated welcome and good day to all of you.

I want to give you all our wholehearted appreciation and thanks for the beautiful and entertaining surprise program, which gave us so much joy and more reason to pray for a longer life in this world, which is full of change and uncertainty.

We felt that we are still noticed and loved, yes we are still considered important to our society, belying our suspicion that we are now just leftovers from the old past days.

From the bottom of our heart, I want to reiterate once more muchas gracias to you beautiful people. Wish you could come again. We will always welcome you with open arms. Your short stay here will always be remembered.

May the Lord bless you and keep you safe as you go through life.

The participants of Golden Acres love you all. Goodbye and good luck, and a safe and happy trip home.

Love, the Golden People from Golden Acres

She had written the note with one of the flower pens we made and gave the residents. I recognized the ink from those pens we had wrapped in green tape with an artificial red rose from Michael's Arts and Crafts. I might have tossed the slip of paper away if she had not put it in my hands. To this day, I still have the note. It remains tucked in a box with other messages and pictures I have received through VAMS. They remind me of the transformative power of helping others.

LESSON 3

Focus on the Big Picture in Civic Work – But Don't Forget the Details

TOM AND ERNESTINE

All too often we have both found that civic leaders use either a civic telescope or civic microscope without recognizing the need for a balanced approach. Some have a grand design for their civic ventures, but ignore the concrete steps that must be taken to achieve that design. Alternatively, some are caught up in the weeds of their program and fail to look far enough ahead to develop both a vision of their civic aims and a realistic plan to achieve those aims.

Ernestine learned this lesson at an early stage in her role as a civic leader. As she recounts in her section of this Lesson, she had committed her nonprofit organization to a Halloween festival that would include many hundreds of people of all ages whom they had been serving, as well as a large group of their student volunteers. The festival was widely publicized with the goal of bringing all these people together and showing their common sense of humanity through sharing music and programs that they could enjoy together. But Ernestine needed a space to hold so many people and their activities. No such space was readily available and she realized that the whole grand scheme, and the many benefits it could promote, would be lost without attention to this detail. Fortunately, she found a space through the generosity of a senior executive at a television studio. But she learned through that experience to take the time and care to work through such details before announcing a dream that might end up as a nightmare.

Tom learned a related lesson, as he tells in his section, when he worked for Under Secretary of State George W. Ball and realized too late that his wife, Ellen, might have inadvertently leaked to a reporter with whom she was having dinner a key detail about the American strategy in the Vietnam War: the start of a major U.S. attack. Everyone knew the broad outlines of the U.S. strategy, but the details were top secret, and when Ellen revealed that Tom was still working with Ball late into the night, the reporter immediately guessed—correctly as it turned out—that an attack was about to be launched. More generally, Tom also saw one president, Jimmy Carter, with whom he worked directly, get much too caught up in the minutia of foreign-aid particulars, while his successor, Ronald Reagan, was too little involved to realize, for example, that some of his key lieutenants were planning and executing an illegal operation to provide support to rebels in Nicaragua. In the pages that follow, we stress ways that civic leaders can keep their eyes on both the big picture and the details, ensuring in the process that those who work with them are prepared to be similarly sensitive.

TOM

Repeatedly during my civic work over the years, and in reading and hearing about the civic work of others, I have come to appreciate the importance of focusing on the big picture. President Carter was justly, in my view, accused of failing to follow this precept, and I saw this failing first-hand when I worked for him, as I'll discuss a bit later. A big-picture focus is important and difficult to achieve when there are powerful pressures pressing in multiple different directions, as is so often the case in civic work. But it is also important, as I came to learn, not to forget the details.

An experience I had when working for Abram Chayes while he was State Department Legal Adviser reinforces that point. McCarthyism was still alive and well in 1962, and charges were frequently made that State Department officials were "soft" on Communism. This was especially true in the office of Abba Schwartz, a good friend of mine and the

Assistant Secretary in charge of passports, visas, and similar matters. The Senate Internal Security Subcommittee was actively engaged in witch-hunting for alleged Communists. The Secretary of State, Dean Rusk, had become increasingly concerned that someone was tapping telephones inside Schwartz's office because confidential comments that he had made on his telephone were regularly the subject of questions by the Senate Subcommittee staff. I was charged with finding out what had happened. A former employee in Schwartz's office was working in our London embassy, and I was dispatched there by Secretary Rusk— with only an hour's notice—to interrogate the former employee. I spent several hours questioning the man in a tiny basement office of the embassy. At the end of the session, I was convinced that, whatever else, this man had not been involved in tapping Schwartz's telephones, and that he knew nothing about anyone else doing so.

To my great embarrassment, a few days later the same man appeared in my Washington office with his lawyer to confess that he and another employee had copies of Schwartz's telephone conversations and had passed them on to the Subcommittee staff. They had not tapped the telephones. Rather, they had planted "bugs," tiny electronic receivers, in the Assistant Secretary's office. In short, I had focused on the big picture, but neglected to pay attention to the details, as my failure to distinguish telephone "bugs" and "wiretaps" makes clear.

Chayes told me in the Spring of 1964 that he would have to return to teaching at Harvard or lose his tenured position there. I immediately thought that I would like to work for George W. Ball, who had been at the State Department since the outset of the Kennedy Administration, first as Under Secretary for Economic Affairs and then as Under Secretary, the second ranking person in the State Department after Secretary Rusk. When Chayes left the State Department I knew that I would soon try teaching law. But since I had come to Washington, I had admired Ball as the best craftsman of policy and words in the State Department. I could not forgo the chance to work for him if he would have me.

So I went to Ball to ask if I might join his office, and he hired me as his assistant. My primary responsibility was to write policy analyses and speeches. In retrospect, it sometimes seems to me that I spent much of the first half of my life writing words for others to say and letters for others to sign, and much of the second half of my life giving speeches that others wrote and signing letters that others prepared. In fact, however, my year with Ball taught me that a good speaker and writer will never simply take the words of another. Rather, at its best, a real partnership develops.

With one exception, I never wrote a single piece of prose for Ball that he did not revise by at least a few words. That one exception, ironically, was a short introduction to a volume titled, *A Practical Guide to Effective Writing* (Random House, 1965). The guide was written by a retired government official who taught writing to others in the government. The substance of what I wrote in that guide was based on lessons I learned from Ball:

> I was taught to believe that the statement of an idea is no less important than the idea itself. Clarity of expression can never replace thought, but no thought can be expressed with full force unless it is clearly stated. Few of us can write gracefully, but all of us can write intelligibly. Yet I have observed both in private and in public life that many papers are written to conceal ideas—or the lack of them— rather than to communicate any thought or purpose.
>
> Those who take pleasure in words and the meanings of words enjoy their use. They find satisfaction in the plain statement of a complex problem. But this virtue seems lacking in the authors of many papers that, over the years, have crossed my desk.
>
> I am dismayed at the inability of people in all walks of life, including the Government, to express themselves. They cross swords with syntax in almost every sentence. They apparently regard the conception that a sentence should have a subject and a predicate as outmoded, if not subversive. I persist in my simple faith that the unadorned declarative sentence is one of man's noblest architectural achievements. But it is also one of his rarest.

Sometimes Ball would draft and I would edit. More often, he would edit my drafts. But either way, we worked together as a team. He had a distinctive voice, a pattern of putting together words and phrases unique to his mind and pen. He cared deeply about words and the meaning of words. His bibles, like Judge Hand's, were Fowler's *Modern English Usage* and *The Elements of Style* by Strunk and White. Ball enjoyed finding the right word for a particular point almost more than knowing whether the point was right.

Ball had a remarkable ability to concentrate on key issues in American foreign policy and to bear down with intensity on those issues. He believed passionately that the future of the United States depended primarily on a close partnership with a united Europe and with Japan. The major enemy was the Soviet Union and the partnership was essential, primarily through NATO, in defending our vital interests. Other matters could be important, but this was the top U.S. priority and he did not want the U.S. in its foreign policy to lose sight of that big picture or to be diverted to less significant concerns.

On one of the trips to Europe when I accompanied Ball, we spent a day talking with Jean Monet, the great architect of the Common Market, and during that day I gained understanding and commitment to the European-American alliance. Ball was much less concerned about relations with developing countries, not because he lacked compassion for those in need of help from the United States. He was strongly supportive of giving that help. Rather, he was concerned that the United States not be diverted from its main foreign-policy objectives. In Ball's view, South Vietnam was a diversion because the U.S. had no dominant interests there or in its survival as a country. For that reason, he thought that the United States involvement in the escalating war between North and South Vietnam was a mistake from the outset. The French had failed there and had been forced to leave. Ball thought we should learn from the mistakes of the French and not get entangled in a war we could never win. He was convinced that the public interest required our prompt withdrawal of military personnel in South Vietnam.

While I was working for Ball, I also learned an important lesson about dealing with reporters. Ellen and I were close friends with the White House reporter for *The New York Times* and his wife. We were scheduled to have dinner at their home one Saturday night, but at the last minute I could not come because of an issue concerning the Vietnam buildup. Ellen innocently told our hosts that I was detained in a meeting with Ball at the Defense Department. Our *New York Times* friend immediately guessed that a rumored U.S. attack on North Vietnam was underway and called his newspaper colleagues to track down the details of the story, which they did. No one learned that Ellen and I were the immediate cause of the "leaked" story, but we learned a valuable lesson—good reporters may also be good friends. But when they smell a story, their journalistic instincts will trump friendship.

When I started working for Ball in June 1964 the United States had military advisers in South Vietnam, but our country had not committed to a significant troop build-up. The Vietnam War was going poorly for South Vietnam and the U.S., however, and President Johnson was considering sending large numbers of troops. General William Westmoreland became head of all U.S. troops there that June.

Much of the year that I worked with Ball was spent in drafting various plans to help the United States extricate itself from South Vietnam. These documents were so sensitive that usually only four copies existed: one for the president, one for Rusk, one for McNamara, and one for Ball. They were responsible for ensuring that no other copies were made. This was, of course, long before the era of the Internet and even before rapid copy machines were common, so secrecy was much easier to maintain than it is today.

Although the huge U.S. troop buildup had not yet started there were increasing pressures from Secretary of Defense Robert McNamara to send more U.S. soldiers there and he was supported by Secretary Rusk and President Johnson's National Security Advisor, McGeorge Bundy. Bill Bundy, brother of McGeorge, was Assistant Secretary of State for Far Eastern Affairs and another advocate for escalating the war. Ball was the only senior official who was a strong opponent.

Early in my time working for Ball, an apparent attack by North Vietnam occurred on a U.S. ship in the Gulf of Tonkin. I worked closely with Ball in drafting a resolution authorizing the use of force against North Vietnam, which was rapidly passed by Congress. The attack was reported to the President and the State Department by the Department of Defense, which claimed no doubt about what had happened. We learned only later, however, that the attack was misreported and the intelligence from the Defense Department about the incident was significantly off-base. McNamara would not have supported retaliation, he later said, if he had known the true facts.

Over the course of the year I was with Ball, I helped to write a series of lengthy secret memoranda to President Johnson spelling out the strongest case we could for why escalation was a mistake. Ball organized an informal group of State Department officers who had similar views and great expertise in Vietnamese and Chinese history and politics. The major argument that was made by the pro-buildup advocates was that Communism, backed by China, would roll over Asia "like dominos" unless the U.S. stopped it in South Vietnam. The Chinese were supporting North Vietnam as a first step, these advocates claimed, in what would become a massive strategic power shift. President Johnson was persuaded by Rusk, McNamara, and a group of generals, along with his own National Security Advisor, McGeorge Bundy, that this argument was correct. Johnson did not want "the dominos to fall" on his watch as President, and he felt that the Vietnam War could derail the War on Poverty unless he acted decisively by sending all the troops that the Pentagon generals wanted.

Ball made the case—forcefully and, in my view, persuasively—that this "dominos" view was the wrong "big picture." He argued that vital United States interests were not at stake in the conflict between North and South Vietnam. To the contrary, our vital interests focused on Europe and Japan, and it was there that our "big picture" future really lay. The French defeat in Vietnam illustrated the difficulty of fighting Vietnamese on their own territory. And the ancient enmity between China and Vietnam meant that Vietnam would never agree to be under Chinese domination any more than it would under U.S. control. These were crucial details that Johnson, Rusk, and McNamara were all overlooking.

One of my last experiences working for Ball was to take a top-secret withdrawal plan to Saigon and to present it to our ambassador and the military leaders there. I was recovering from the flu when I boarded a plane for the long flight that took me to Bangkok. I recall getting on Pan American Flight 1 from Washington and falling promptly asleep for most of the next twelve hours. Then I climbed in a fighter plane for an ear-popping trip across Cambodia and Vietnam to Saigon. Unfortunately, my trip failed; the U.S. military and civilian leaders there, led by then Ambassador Maxwell D. Taylor, who had been Chairman of the Joint Chiefs of Staff, were adamant that more U.S. troops were the only answer, and President Johnson accepted their judgment.

In urging U.S. troop withdrawal from Vietnam, Ball was a great international lawyer arguing his case for the public interest before the chief judge on the issue: President Johnson. And Ball was as brilliant an advocate as I have ever seen in action. Johnson listened carefully to him. He took seriously the arguments that Ball was making. But the President ultimately came to rely on McNamara and the generals on the one hand, and McGeorge Bundy and Rusk on the other, and to view

Ball as a "devil's advocate." By the time I left Ball to start teaching at Stanford Law School in June 1965, it was clear that Ball would not succeed. And, in fact, in the Summer and Fall of 1965 the U.S. troop escalation continued at an accelerating pace.

History has shown to all but a small minority that Ball was right and McNamara was wrong. But McNamara was an extraordinarily persuasive advocate who could cite statistics with ease and effectiveness to support his case, and he marshaled a potent array of generals as well. Like Ball, he was able to focus on the big picture, but in the case of Vietnam he failed to acknowledge the key details that made a U.S. defeat inevitable.

I later had the good fortune to work with McNamara when he was head of the World Bank and I was in charge of foreign-aid policies for President Carter. I watched McNamara's remarkable abilities marshaled to promote long-term economic development. But in the Vietnam War he was tragically wrong, as he himself came to understand; much too late in terms of the lives that were lost and the billions of wasted dollars that were spent.

McNamara's failure in one realm of his civic work—the Vietnam War—and his success in another—the World Bank—underscore an obvious caveat that must be added to Lesson 2, "Civic Work Must Serve the Public Interest." In both situations, McNamara was passionately convinced that he was serving the public interest. His human flaws led to his failure to appreciate that his actions jeopardized rather than supported American security and caused appalling losses of lives, both Vietnamese and American, in the process. He lacked the skepticism that marked, in different ways, both Hand and Ball, and instead had a headstrong certitude in terms of his own military beliefs when facing an enemy unlike any America had faced before. And he lived to realize his tragic errors in leading our country into the Vietnam War. But he, too, like Hand, Chayes, and Ball, did his best to serve the public interest, and it is important not to confuse right judgment with dedicated civic service.

ERNESTINE

While a student at Stanford, I volunteered to participate in student government and on various University committees. In these roles, I came to appreciate the importance of finding the right balance in civic work between considering the big picture and paying close attention to details.

Near the end of my sophomore year, I was elected to serve for one year as a student representative to the Board of Trustees, and as a voting member on its Committee on Land and Buildings. This was a time when a number of buildings were being designed and constructed at the University. I took part in reviewing plans for a diverse array of new facilities, including a home for the Department of Art and Art History, a Campus Energy System Improvements project to meet the University's energy needs through 2050, and a structure to house a major art collection that had just been given to the University. My role on the Board was especially interesting for me, as I was the only undergraduate representative to the Committee on Land and Buildings of the Board, which has fiduciary responsibilities for governing the University. I had been a student for many years, but had never been in a position to view the operations of an educational institution from the vantage point of its governing body.

My experience with Stanford's Board of Trustees was entirely different than my involvement with student government. Sitting in a board room at a building for student organizations every Tuesday evening, my fellow peers and I would often argue over a significant issue for a time and then switch to what seemed the most minor of concerns. We would worry about major matters such as eliminating line items that we felt were superfluous in the budgets of student groups, struggle over how to increase awareness of the counseling and psychological services at the University's Allene G. Vaden Health Center, and make recommendations for engaging students in the Career Development Center's alumni mentoring program. But we also spent a significant amount of time parsing detailed documents, many of which were more complex than what I had worked on in my writing courses at Stanford. We sometimes debated whether to revise a single word or how best to condense unnecessary text. We occasionally even argued about aligning bullet points.

At first, I thought this concentration on details would be absent when I served on the Board of Trustees, which has responsibilities for decisions about broad aspects of University affairs. But over time I learned that in making those decisions, we frequently needed to consider seemingly small technicalities. My study of details, perfected at the level of student government, facilitated my abilities to participate in the decision-making processes of the Trustees along with the members of the Board and senior University administrators.

This Asian proverb has been rephrased many times: "The frog in the well knows not of the great ocean." For me, the proverb means that details are important, but sometimes you need to take a step back and examine the bigger picture, while retaining a strong understanding of the specifics. It is important to find the right balance. My work with student government prepared me for my role on the Board, for that role required me to maintain a broad perspective on the University's welfare, since the decisions we made directly influenced major aspects of University affairs, while reminding me that I should be mindful of the details of those decisions.

From my work on both bodies, I also learned that what might seem like a detail to one person may be an essential element in the bigger picture for another. What do I mean by "the big picture?" Goals often vary, and through my experiences with the Trustees, it also became clear to me that people define the big picture in different ways, often depending on their own backgrounds.

On materials for meetings of the Committee on Land and Buildings, under the Stanford emblem in the upper left corner, I frequently wrote the word "sustainability" or some variation of it in my notebook. For me, the big picture was how to create a sustainable built environment for the University. It was a particular interest of mine and a focus of my undergraduate major. Stanford should, I believed, not just construct more facilities, but build ones that were ecologically sound. For others on the Committee, the big picture was primarily about constructing buildings of the highest quality architectural design. For still others, the key focus was on costs.

Likewise, the scores of different youth with whom Tom and I spoke about their civic work defined the big picture in many different ways. Sean Russell is one example. I first met Sean through the State Farm® Youth Advisory Board, on which I was selected to serve during the summer after my senior year of high school. State Farm® allocates five million dollars of its philanthropic giving each year to the Board. It is responsible for administering grants for youth-led service-learning projects throughout North America. Thirty students serve on the Board, and together they decide how to distribute grants among competing proposals. One of the best things about the Youth Advisory Board, or the "YAB" as we affectionately like to call ourselves, is the opportunity to build a strong, personal relationship with civic leaders across the United States and Canada.

In Florida, Sean started a "Stow It—Don't Throw It" project to encourage recycling and to discourage careless disposal of monofilament fishing line and other marine debris. In working on this project, the big picture for Sean was bringing together people of all ages to recycle. I had a chance to hear about the impact of Sean's civic work at a marina in Florida, during a King Fish Tournament.

As he told me his story, I imagined boats of all sizes gliding into the harbor, disturbing the water and creating gentle ripples. A golden circle formed on the water, expanding as the sun passed below the horizon. Friends and family stood at the shoreline, watching boats drift in and bring in fish to weigh. On the dock, Sean was also waiting for the fishermen to come in. Sitting at his wooden display booth, he noticed a young girl. "Do you fish?" he asked the young girl with caramel-brown hair that formed a heart around her face. She nodded. Sean passed her a personal sized fishing line recycling bin made from a recycled tennis ball can. It was boldly labeled: "Stow It—Don't Throw It." Sean beamed as he watched the young girl clip the recycling bin to her belt buckle before running to meet her dad, one of the competing fishermen. Her dad, whose hair was a bit lighter in color, and tousled with waves, had just stepped off his boat. He, like his daughter, also had a recycling bin clipped on his belt loop. Both father and daughter had committed to becoming responsible anglers, and that gave Sean a deep sense of satisfaction.

Sean had started "Stow It-Don't Throw It" when he began collaborating with youth in Florida's 4-H program and an older scientist who led a dolphin research project at Mote Marine Laboratory in Sarasota, Florida. He involves youth and adults of all ages through school programs, summer camps, and a variety of environmental organizations.

They all work together to further the cause of responsible angling practices and the prevention of marine debris.

Sean shared with me how important it is to bring together people of all ages in civic work. "It's not just about youth involvement without any adult support," he said, "It's also not about a civic organization run by grownups." It is about bringing together people for a good cause— young people, old people, everyone.

Alex Wirth was another fellow Board member from the State Farm® Youth Advisory Board. For him, the big picture was to listen carefully to the people he was trying to help in his civic work. He became an advocate for youth involvement and served on youth councils for DoSomething.org and Youth Service America, two national organizations that help teenage youth find civic work that matches their passions.

Alex told me about the Department of Education's first National Youth Summit, where he volunteered to moderate a workshop with three senior government officials and thirty students. They were part of an event involving hundreds of youth participants, spanning various parts of the country. He recalled pacing around with a microphone, taking questions—question after question, hand after hand after hand. So many youth were trying to speak, trying to make their voices heard. Alex took on the role of being sure that each student felt that his or her voice was being heard by the group and that, whenever possible, individuals with like interests could connect together.

One student who stood out, Alex told me, was an African American boy. He was from the Bronx. As the meeting got underway, the boy seemed unusually frustrated, impatiently shuffling in his seat with one hand waving impatiently. His hand was up for quite a while before Alex called on him. "How do we know this isn't a show?" he burst out.

It was then that Alex realized, more vividly than ever before, that the participating youth didn't just want to attend a summit. They weren't just there to talk for a day before retreating to their respective communities. They wanted their opinions to be heard in ways that would be acted on. From that experience, Alex reminded me of an important aspect of public service: You have to listen carefully to people you are trying to help. Let them sit around the table and create change with you. As my friend Tim Hsia, who went to the United States Military

Academy at West Point and served in Iraq, told me, "Get to know people on a one-on-one basis. Know what they're going through."

I have been rejected numerous times, and people have not always listened or acknowledged me. I remember my heart pounding with mixed feelings of excitement and fear when I walked into the Northridge Recreation Center office and rapidly blabbered, "Hi, I'm Ernestine Fu, founder and president of Visual Arts and Music for Society." The manager took a quick up-down glance at me, and asked, "How old are you again?" Before I could respond, he brusquely explained that the Center typically did not deal with individuals as young as I was, that I did not have the necessary permits, and that the facility could not be put at risk by accommodating the "unruly children" who were my volunteers. I walked away dejected.

Later, I laughed to myself at his comment on "unruly children." He had no idea what "unruly children" meant. I thought about the children I had already encountered through VAMS. There was Brittany, a two-year old with large aquamarine eyes, pudgy cheeks, and smooth skin with red patches spattered across half her face and down parts of her neck. With a huge smile she once commanded me to eat a cookie with creamy chocolate frosting on top and hard, tangy candy mixed with chewy marshmallows throughout. When I ate it, the sides of my mouth were lined with red frosting and cookie crumbs, and my stomach throbbed in sugar overload. But Brittany had a big smile on her face as she held half of another cookie inches away from my mouth, forcing my lips open. This one was topped with icing one inch high and covered with all twelve toppings we had placed on the table. She had already gobbled down her half of the cookie. As I chewed, forcing myself to swallow and lick the excess frosting from my lips, Brittany grinned with a wide smile that scrunched her cheeks, accentuating the pudginess and forming crows' feet around the red splotches near her eyes. Brittany and others like her—those were unruly children. I focused on experiences like the one with Brittany as I approached Michael Klausman, president of CBS Studio Center, a couple weeks later.

It was August of 2008, two months before the Annual VAMS Halloween Spooktacular, and I desperately needed a space that would accommodate over five hundred orphans, foster care children, and homeless families, as well as one hundred volunteers. Our volunteers had planned this event for months, and we intended something bigger and better than what we had ever done before. Luckily, an award-winning writer, actor, author, and early supporter of my civic work, Bruce Neckels, put me in touch with Mr. Klausman.

I feared I would receive another hostile reaction when I was escorted past two bulky security guards and up an extensive set of stairs to meet Mr. Klausman. As I walked into his office, I noticed dozens of impressive plaques, awards, and trophies and the faint sound of CBS News on Channel 2 playing in the corner, and thought, "This guy's a big shot. There's no way he'll support me." I expected Mr. Klausman and CBS Studios to give me another curt rejection. Luckily, I was wrong.

Mr. Klausman sat behind a black wooden executive desk, casually peering up from his work as I walked in. He is a lean man with neatly parted dark gray hair and square glasses. When I nervously stepped into his office, he sat patiently with a stoic, solemn expression as I pulled out various colorful brochures and crinkled local newspaper articles to explain VAMS' goals and recent activities. As I briefly paused to hear his opinion, he casually broke his solemn look, smiled, and asked something along the lines of, "So what do you want from me?" "I'd like your New York Street film lot for my upcoming VAMS Halloween Spooktacular event. We really need a space for over 500 orphans, foster care children, and homeless families. I can't afford to rent a venue," I responded. He grinned and said, "Sure, let's do it."

As I came to learn, the big picture to Mike Klausman is to treat everyone with compassion and respect. My friend, Marta Hanson, has a favorite quote that describes Mr. Klausman's viewpoint: "To the world you may be one person, but to one person you may be the world."

Marta Hanson had the opportunity to design and teach a "Random Act of Kindness" workshop for middle-school students in the Bay Area. The workshop was held in a classroom full of twelve and thirteen year olds. During one session that she told me about, a particular student stood out — a boy with long, unkempt black hair, jeans that were torn in seemingly random areas, and a black T-shirt that hugged his gaunt body. His features made him conspicuous, but his location obscured him. He sat in the back of the room, tucked away in a corner near the window, and despite the occasional rocking of his chair, he could have continued on through the workshop unobserved. That is, if he had been quiet. Despite his half-hidden location, John made sure everyone recognized his presence. When John first sauntered into the class, Marta sensed trouble. "Why is he here? Did his mom force him to come here?" she thought.

These thoughts continued to float around Marta's head as she began distributing "Kindness Kits", legal-sized manila envelope that each contained a colorful pack of post-it notes, stamped envelopes, stickers, and other paraphernalia. "Sharing is caring: eat one for yourself, and give one to someone else," read the green sticker card that tied together two pieces of fun-sized Milky Way chocolates in each kit. John was the first to rip open the candy and chomp it down. But he didn't just eat one; he ate both. He then proceeded to proclaim loudly, his voice resonating from the back of the room to the front, "This is silly! Why would I want to do a nice thing for someone else? I won't do any of this." Marta recalled what her mother, a teacher, had often told her, "Don't go into a classroom assuming who the good kids are and who the bad kids are." Marta hesitated before ignoring John and continuing on with the class.

Marta described the power of acting kindly even to strangers, from blowing up red and pink balloons on Valentine's Day and randomly tying them onto bikes, to seeing an encouraging post-it note on the bathroom mirror when she herself was feeling down. "You are beautiful," it read. "What have I done for others, strangers?" Marta encouraged the students to ponder and then to draw on their stack of post-its.

During this quiet drawing period, Marta and the three student volunteers each individually approached John, consciously attempting to treat this "stranger" with dignity and respect, simply like an adult, although he was only twelve years old. As they took turns sitting beside him, the volunteers slowly noticed a change in his demeanor, a gradual transition from cocky coolness to a genuinely sheepish nature. "You're taking me seriously? You respect me as a person even though I'm only half your age?" his face read.

At the end of the session, John approached Marta and her volunteers. "I made this for you," he shyly whispered, tilting his head and searching their faces for some sort of approval. It was a pink post-it note with each of their names on it, intricately surrounded by a border of doodles.

Marta shared with me the importance of treating everyone, from the rude twelve year-old to the homeless man on the streets, with respect. Your presumptions, she told me, often guide the individual behavior of others. Think, she said, about people whom you have met in your life who seemed to repel you, so you pushed them away. Next time, she urged, give them another chance. That was her big picture.

One summer, I found myself wearing a black and white shirt that read "UCLA" and "VAMS." We didn't have enough money for colored shirts. It was my junior year of high school, and I had decided to gather a group of my friends and dedicated volunteers from the VAMS organization for what became the VAMS Youth Leadership Seminar at UCLA, a conference that brought together almost a hundred high-school students to learn about broader goals of VAMS. I remember sharing with the Seminar attendees the big picture for VAMS. As I told them, the people who hear the music we make are fellow humans, yet too often they have little pleasure in their lives that are full of physical and mental challenges. They know too rarely, if at all, what joy music can bring, particularly music played by musicians who are standing or sitting in front of them with instruments to communicate directly via one universal language: music. I also shared memories of my own civic work that have and will always remain with me. There's the satisfaction of seeing an ecstatic little girl dancing despite a broken arm, a young boy with a cleft palate squeezing out a tiny smile when I make him an origami spider, a teenage foster girl wrapping her arms around me as we look through pictures, a senior citizen nodding to the beat of our jazz music, and a joyful girl receiving a huge stuffed teddy bear. These memories—scores and scores of details—have become a part of who I am. Along with the civic work that accompanied them, they became an integral part of my identity.

Near the end of the Seminar, I remember sitting with my sister, Christine, at a table in the back. We had draped a long banquet table with red tablecloths and proclaimed it the "Judge's Table." Twirling my pencil and fidgeting with the evaluation form in front of me, I sat reflecting on the day, reflecting on the conference and all the energy it took. Small details consumed the days leading up to the Seminar: treading up and down the aisles of Staples to find enough colored folders to represent the different student teams, struggling my way through Photoshop and Adobe InDesign to create nametags on my dad's 1998 computer, biking to the post office two blocks from my house to mail packets for our guest speakers, standing in front of my bathroom mirror to practice my opening speech, over and over again. But as I snapped photos of students presenting their final projects that day, I was once again reminded of the big picture of the Seminar: helping a group of youth to gain the knowledge, skills, and enthusiasm to create positive change when they returned to their communities.

Today, I still get a special feeling when I receive letters from those with whom I have engaged in civic work. I like mementos that remind me of joy and struggle, the long journey I have taken as a public servant. I often pin their notes on my wall, on a large corkboard about the size of my desk, alongside photos with multiple holes from having been pinned and re-pinned. One photo has followed me from Southern California to my various college dorm rooms, remaining on my bulletin board throughout the years. It is a photo of the staff at that first Seminar I organized one summer in high school. I am sitting on a concrete bench with student volunteers on my left, right, and behind me. Sunlight shines brightly on our faces, highlighting our features, our foreheads slightly glistening. We are all smiling, that smile that comes right after a laugh.

LESSON 4

Motives to Engage in Civic Work Are Always Mixed

TOM AND ERNESTINE

We have explained that civic work should always serve the public interest. In this Lesson, we add an important corollary: that serving the public interest need not be the only motive for civic work. In reality, it is usually impossible to separate the multiple motives that lead to action on behalf of a civic cause. Tom was inspired by the civic work of both his parents. Ernestine found that her flute playing eased her sister's depression, and this was a primary reason she founded a nonprofit organization.

We have both been blessed in that while we did not come from backgrounds of wealth, we had the good fortune to receive outstanding educations, which also contributed directly to our motivations for civic work. While Ernestine grew up in Los Angeles where the education standards in public schools were weak, she had the good fortune to be chosen for a magnet program that provided a free education with superb courses taught by excellent teachers. Tom was lucky to have had an Exeter Academy education, thanks to his grandmother's financial support. Exeter was, in his view, the most important educational schooling of his life, more significant than either Harvard College or Harvard Law School. At Exeter, "Non Sibi"—not for self—was the school motto, and in the crucial transition period between adolescence and adult-

hood, the meaning of that motto in action became part of Tom's identity.

We certainly benefited enormously in our civic work as a result of
those educations. But our educations at elite schools should not be seen
as a limitation on the angles of vision about civic work in this book.
Many of those whose stories we tell of successful civic work were much
less fortunate than we were in their educations.

We stress that while we were exposed to some of the best education
in both high school and college, this is not a prerequisite to civic work.
Various circumstances, as we outline in this Lesson, can also drive civic
work that makes major differences in the lives of others and in a community.

TOM

I frequently hear young people tell me that they have volunteered for
some civic activity in part because they think it will "look good on their
college applications." I sometimes meet people my age who sheepishly
confess to me that they are civic volunteers as a way to meet new
friends. In both cases, the suggestion is implied that only pure altruism
is a valid basis for civic work. In my experience, mixed motives are
normal, and one should not apologize for having them.

In the Fall of 1942, the efforts to mobilize our country to fight World
War II were well underway. I was eight years old, and was consumed by
stories and pictures of America's fighting soldiers and sailors. My family
and I were living in Washington, D.C., where we had just moved so that
my father could work at the Office of Price Administration, which had
control over the prices of goods and services. He had previously worked
in a Boston department store, but he wanted to be involved in civic
work and I was proud of him for doing so.

I wanted to do my part as well. This certainly included plastering the
walls of my room with pictures of U.S. Navy ships and Air Force planes.
But I wanted to do more. I wanted to contribute directly to helping the
war effort.

I thought I had my chance when the neighborhood movie theater
advertised that it would give free admission at the Saturday morning
double-feature to anyone bringing five pounds or more of scrap iron to

donate for use in making bullets and battleships. I loved the movies and was particularly entranced by this theater's fare on Saturday mornings, which was always a war movie, a Western, and multiple cartoons. My friends and I would arrive a bit before the 10:00 a.m. start time and not leave until mid-afternoon.

But where to find the five pounds of metal that I needed as the price of admission? Why, the iron used for pressing clothes in our home seemed perfect. It was made of iron and weighed at least five pounds. I did not bother to check with my mother, but instead grabbed the iron and lugged it to the movie theater where I met my friends and gained admission. Did I honestly believe my mother would be pleased at my display of civic virtue? I am not sure, though I know that by the time I returned home that afternoon I was convinced that I had done a fine thing for our country's war effort as well as seen two great movies.

That night my mother asked how I had gotten into the movies with no money, and I reported that I had donated our family's iron as a contribution to fighting Germany and Japan. My mother was furious. Needless to say, our family had only one iron and it was gone, with no possibility of replacing it until the war was over. My mother immediately marched me down to the movie theater, went directly to the manager, and somehow succeeded in retrieving the iron. And, as punishment, I was deprived of any movies for the rest of the fall.

My mother was right, of course. Yet in thinking back on that experience, I see it as the first of numerous occasions when I have tried to further some civic value that I thought important while simultaneously promoting more personal interests or ambitions. Most of the time, I hope that I have done so with a bit more wisdom than I showed in my initial foray into civic life. But a mixture of motives has been a constant.

This is a book about the importance of furthering civic values and about sound approaches that can engage young people in developing those values. I believe deeply that civic work is a noble calling and that, whether the work is full-time or part-time, as an avocation or a vocation, it can be enormously rewarding in terms of personal satisfaction. The civic work may be tutoring a single child—as my wife, Ellen, has done and as Ernestine's friend Patrick had done—or it may be teaching full-time in a public school, as Ellen also did, or serving part-time on a school board, which is civic work undertaken by many of my friends across the country. In two prior books that I wrote with Anne Colby,

Educating Citizens: Preparing America's Undergraduates for Lives of Moral and Civic Responsibility (Jossey-Bass, 2003) and *Educating for Democracy: Preparing Undergraduates for Responsible Political Engagement* (Jossey-Bass, 2007) we discuss why education for good citizenship should involve learning more than just individual civic activities like helping in a community kitchen. It should also include promoting systemic improvement in the civic life of one's community, local, state, national, or even international. This means learning why the community has such a kitchen and what it will take, as a matter of public policy, to ensure that the kitchen is no longer needed.

I do not suggest, however, that youth or anyone else should be involved in promoting civic ends solely for altruistic reasons. Few of us engage in helping others just to be good citizens with no thought of what our actions do for ourselves or our reputations with others. To the contrary, a mix of reasons is generally what propels us to act or not to act, and the civic arena in this respect is no different than others.

There are "testing cases," of course, when the civic or altruistic motive may be far heavier on the scale than any others. Our synagogue in Los Altos, California, has a "tzedakah box" in which we are encouraged to put totally anonymous donations for some worthy charity that changes each month. No one knows what we are giving or even whether we are giving at all. But each of us knows what we do, and most of the time someone close to us—a spouse or child, for example—knows as well. It certainly makes us feel good to donate in this fashion, and we may think it will serve as an instructive lesson to our child who sees us do so. It is no less worthy because we have such mixed motives.

Similarly, when we donate blood through the Red Cross, we know we are helping others though most of the time we do not know who will be the recipients of our blood. The Red Cross takes a variety of steps to encourage our donations, including the assurance that should we need a blood transfusion in the future, the Red Cross will provide it. We also may receive a pin or other tangible sign to others that we have donated blood. Again, these benefits do not make our donation any the less an act of civic virtue.

My own initial forays into full-time civic work were similarly the results of mixed motives, as well as luck. As I've written, after I finished Harvard Law School, I spent an extraordinary year as law clerk for one of the nation's most renowned federal judges, Learned Hand. I was offered the clerkship by great good fortune. It was the spring of my third year at Harvard Law School. My wife, Ellen, and I had been married for two years and we were expecting our first child in the fall. I had clearly in mind that I eventually wanted to teach law, but I thought that I should have some experience in practicing law since the overwhelming majority of my students would be law practitioners.

In fact, I had decided that I wanted to be a teacher well before I decided to go to law school. My mother claims that I made this decision in the second grade because of my infatuation with my teacher at the time, who had a wonderfully "everyman" name: Mrs. Scattergood. One day that year I came home from school and started calling my mother "Mrs. Scattergood." This hardly pleased my mother, as anyone can imagine, but from then on she said she knew that I would be a teacher.

My own sense is that it was the extraordinary teachers—as Ernestine and I discuss in Lesson 1—with whom I had early contact that shaped my decision to make teaching a career. My choice of law was shaped, at least initially, by a biography of Justice Louis Brandeis that my grandmother gave me to read. She was a widow by the time I was in high school, and whenever possible I would have lunch with her on Saturdays. Invariably, she gave me a book that she had read and thought I would like. I would read the book before our next lunch and we would talk about it. Though she had only a high-school education, she was extraordinarily well read and encouraged me to read widely in history and literature. The Thomas Adolphus Mason biography of Brandeis—I can still see that blue-cloth bound volume—made an enormous impact on me. It opened my thoughts to how a gifted lawyer could help shape society. While I knew I would be no Brandeis, I wanted to use my intellect for the public good as he had done.

The thought of being a judicial law clerk, however, was not in my mind in the Spring of 1959 as I was about to graduate from Harvard Law School. Instead, Ellen and I were planning to move to Milwaukee where we would start raising our family, and I would practice law for a couple of years and then look for a law teaching job. I had already accepted a job with a Milwaukee firm, Foley & Lardner, where I would be going with several of my classmates, for we had decided that it would be fun to practice together. The firm was one of only two in the country we could find that would hire us together. We were all on the *Harvard Law Review* and thought this approach to hiring made lots of sense, though only one other law firm, Jones Day in Cleveland, agreed to employ all of us. And in the end we decided, as a group, to join Foley & Lardner.

One day that spring, Professor Livingston Hall, a teacher at Harvard Law School, asked me to come see him. He told me that Judge Hand looked to him to recommend a law clerk each year and Professor Hall said he wanted to recommend me. Ellen and I discussed this new possibility and quickly decided that it would be a great opportunity and so I accepted.

My motives were mixed. On the one hand, I knew that being law clerk for one of the country's greatest jurists would be a chance to engage in public service full-time, perhaps the only chance I would have. This was one motive. But another, no less strong, was my realization that working with one of the country's greatest jurists would give me an important window into the judiciary, and that this window would be enormously helpful in gaining and retaining a job in law teaching, where so much of the intellectual work was analyzing judicial court opinions.

My next opportunity for full-time civic work came two years later, in 1962. John F. Kennedy was president. Ellen and I were both exhilarated by his abilities to lead an administration that appealed to the highest ideals of civic work. I had been actively involved in Democratic politics for the past decade, since Adlai Stevenson had been the losing presidential candidate in 1952 while I was a freshman at Harvard College. Stevenson inspired me with his abilities as an orator and his intellect. He brought to his role as Governor of Illinois and candidate for the U.S. presidency a probing mind that saw multiple sides of every policy issue. Though he was often criticized in subsequent years as being indecisive, in my mind—now as then—he was a wise analyst in both domestic and international affairs, and a civic model to me.

During my college years at Harvard, I had been head of the Democratic Club, which was my first introduction to political life. In that role, I invited to campus various speakers. One of them was James Michael Curley, the infamous and once-jailed mayor of Boston. Curley accepted my invitation and his speech was scheduled one weekday at 4:00 p.m. in Sanders Theater, then the largest auditorium at Harvard, and an overflow crowd arrived there early. I had agreed with Curley's staff that I would meet his car outside the auditorium. When 4:00 p.m. came and

Curley had not arrived, I was worried. At 4:30 p.m. I raced to a phone and called his office. "Why he is there with you," I was told by one of his assistants. It took most of the next hour before I found out that he had been diverted by a group of pranksters from the *Harvard Lampoon*, the college humor magazine, who took Curley into the Lampoon building, locked him inside and then left. They thought this was incredibly funny, and in retrospect I think it was pretty amusing as well. But, needless to say, I did not think so at the time. Nor did the Mayor. I was fortunate not to have been blackballed forever from Democratic politics.

My first position in civic work after college, as a summer speechwriter for Foster Furcolo, the Democratic gubernatorial candidate in Massachusetts, was gained thanks to the recommendation of one of my professors at Harvard. When Furcolo was elected, he asked me to join his office as a speechwriter before starting Harvard Law School the next fall. These experiences gave me my initial direct contact with public policy and the sense of satisfaction that comes with contributing to the resolutions of policy issues. I came to learn what pleasures can be gained from grappling with a tough problem facing part of the public and from working collaboratively with interest groups, legislators, and other government officials to help ameliorate, if not resolve, that problem.

In January 1961, after law school and my clerkship with Judge Hand, I was practicing law in Milwaukee. John F. Kennedy gave his inauguration speech that month and I was enormously moved by his words. Years later, as chair of the Commission on National and Community Service, I helped prepare a report titled, "What you can do for your country…" which is, of course, taken from the most memorable line in that memorable speech. But my wife, Ellen, and I had a child in 1961, and I might not have left private law practice for full-time civic work had not another fortuity occurred.

This time my good fortune came through another of my teachers at Harvard Law School, Abram Chayes. I had come to know Chayes as a student at Harvard Law School and had done well in his course on advanced corporation law. As a law teacher, Chayes was the perfect Socratic questioner, always responding to a student's answer with a question. Most of his course was spent on arcane legal problems relating to dividends. But the substance of the issues did not much matter. The course was really about legal analysis—taking a problem, breaking it into its component parts, and then putting them back together again with new insight. My classmates and I learned from Chayes the ability to examine problems closely and from all sides.

Chayes came to Milwaukee to give a speech, and although I was not able to go, Ellen did attend and talked with him afterward. "Why don't you and Tom come to Washington," he asked her, "and Tom could be my special assistant?" Ellen brought this news home that night, and we discussed the matter. I knew I would not continue much longer in private law practice, but did it make sense to postpone my quest for a law-teaching job? I had already received one faculty offer, from North-western Law School, but had turned it down on the ground that I needed more practical experience. A move to the State Department would be a real diversion from my expected career plan. And the salary, I learned when I talked with Chayes, would be less than two-thirds of what I was making as an associate in the law firm. But what an opportunity! Could I really turn it down?

For guidance, I turned to one of the young partners at the law firm where I worked. I knew he was eager to join the Kennedy administration and had just been offered the position of General Counsel to the Comptroller of the Currency. He was thrilled by the offer and eager to accept. When I told him of Chayes' proposal, he quickly urged me to decline. "Wait at least five years until you are a partner in this firm," he said. "Then you can take a leave to go into government and come back when the administration changes in Washington." Later that week, he went to the senior partner in the firm to ask for a leave himself and for some financial support while he was away since the government job would pay only a fraction of what he was then earning. The senior partner stunned him by saying that he would not be granted a leave, that if he left he could not be assured of a place in the law firm when he wanted to return, and that the firm certainly would not subsidize him while he was away. The young partner was heartsick when he reported this to me and said he had reluctantly decided that he could not finan-cially afford to go to Washington.

This coincidental set of circumstances helped convince Ellen and me that we should leave for Washington. We both knew that we did not want ever to become so accustomed to a life style that we could not afford to do something I really wanted to do professionally solely for financial reasons. We probably would have gone to Washington in any event for I was thrilled by the prospect of serving in the Kennedy administration and collaborating closely with a former teacher whom I much admired. And I also thought that a time working in the federal government could help me when I did decide to become a law teacher. In short, my motives were mixed. What I did not realize was that when I finally left government service, in the summer of 1964, for my first teaching job at Stanford Law School, it would be to teach international law and that I would write my first books with Chayes as well. Nor did I know that my work with George W. Ball on the Cyprus crisis would prepare me to write my first law-review article as a Stanford professor, which I later expanded into another book.

None of these decisions that Ellen and I made, and that ultimately led us to Washington, were made purely for the altruistic motive of serving our country. All of them were rooted in mixed motives of personal ambition fused with the desire to help our nation. But, with few exceptions, this is true of every step by every person along the way to engaging in civic work. The reality of mixed motives makes the civic work no less valuable both to the person involved and the community served.

ERNESTINE

As Tom and I discuss in the first lesson, mentors are key in developing a person's public service journey and often in encouraging that person to become initially engaged in public work. Sometimes it is not an individual mentor or teacher who sparks involvement in civic work, but rather a problem that smacks one in the face and cries out for an individual to do something, as Tom and I frequently heard when we met with young people in focus groups to discuss their civic work and their reasons for engaging in that work. These sessions have helped me realize that individuals engage in civic work for many reasons. While my own trying but illuminating experience with my sister Christine was the driving factor in my initial engagement in civic work, it was not the sole factor. Growing up near the downtrodden parts of Los Angeles, I was exposed both to need and to opportunity to help others at an early age. A combination of this environment and Christine's depression drove me to engage in public service and make it a life-long commitment.

From elementary to high school, I was a student in the Los Angeles public education system. For most of my time there, I was in the Highly Gifted Magnet program. As a result, many of my instructors held Ph.D.s and almost all were excellent teachers. But the program was nestled within schools whose walls were sprayed with graffiti, ceilings hung with pencils that had been defiantly thrown upward like missiles, and bathroom stalls that were filled with crude comments scribbled on toilet seats. Drinking, smoking, and skipping class were all part of the environment.

Once in middle school, I was sitting with a couple friends behind the backstop of our baseball field, in a corner sheltered by bushes and trees. As we chatted, Rachel pulled out a small cluster of marijuana leaves. The dark green matched the foliage stuck in the woven metal fence behind us. Casually breaking off clumps of the herb and grinding it with her fingertips, she shoved the flakes into a glass pipe whose sides were lined with burnt ashes. Lighting the pipe, Rachel allowed thin wisps of smoke to emerge, forming "O"s that floated through the metal bars and hoops that decorated her ears, eyebrows, tongue, and wrists. Though I had only known Rachel for only a couple weeks, it was already clear that she was resistant to authority, while at the same time, she maintained a nonchalant attitude towards life. I liked her adventurous spirit, but, sadly, I learned the most from her when she became too daring in the wrong ways.

Minutes after her lighter touched the pipe, creating a pungent smell, a group of gym teachers walked towards us. Rachel threw both lighter and pipe into a bush across the fence, and reached through a diamond-shaped gap to bury the evidence in the leaves. Another student we didn't know had seen the incident and told the teachers. "What are you girls doing? Empty your pockets and remove your shoes," one teacher said as he proceeded to search us.

Rachel pulled out a pack of gum and began furiously chewing. Her breath had reeked of marijuana. "You girls can go," the teacher said, "Except Rachel—you stay." But by the time the school administrators arrived, they could find no evidence of her wrongdoing.

A couple days later, however, the school investigated Rachel again. This time, police had proof that she was receiving drugs and questioned her in an empty classroom about how she obtained them. Although they quickly identified the source, Rachel continued to experiment with drugs for the rest of the year. I lost touch with her when I graduated from middle school, but heard rumors that she had become an active drug dealer.

My high school environment was no less harsh than the middle school's. Outside of the magnet program, pregnant girls strolled the hallways, bathrooms reeked of marijuana, and condoms casually decorated the stairs. Growing up in these grim surroundings exposed me to the harsher elements of life at an early age. When I revisited my high school during a spring break, almost two years after graduating, the first thing I heard when walking down hallways was a white girl yell, "It's like Africa and Mexico—Afrixo in here. Bitches need to get out." There was also that distinct scent reminiscent of the baseball fields where Rachel roamed at my middle school. I saw that not much had changed. Later, upon chatting with students like Christina Chica, the then-current VAMS co-president of North Hollywood High School, I realized that this harsh environment had also influenced others to engage in public service.

For Christina, although she grew up regularly visiting displays at the Getty Museum and attending music shows at the Dorothy Chandler Pavilion, it was not uncommon for her parents to mention someone they knew who was pregnant, using drugs, or even going to jail. One story Christina told me was of her own uncle, who became addicted to drugs and alcohol. Her uncle had worked for several years at restaurants, washing and drying dishes, balancing plates like a circus act, and running errands simply to make ends meet. His earnings were minimal.

Impatient with his lack of money, he began dabbling in the illegal Mexican drug trade. Money soon flowed in, and he quickly became wealthy. With his newly earned, quick and easy money from illegal cartels, he unfortunately began experimenting with the very illegal drugs that he sold. As he spent more and more money on drugs for himself, the savings he had accumulated over several years of hard work dwindled away.

After months of drug and alcohol abuse, Christina's uncle was forced into rehabilitation. "You'll die if you take another sip of alcohol," a doctor said. "Your liver can't handle it anymore." And, in fact, he died soon thereafter.

These grim tales about her uncle and others like him exposed Christina to a reality beyond her family's privileged life, and prompted her to engage in civic work. As she later recounted to me, although her parents didn't tell her right then and there that she should aid people in need, their conversations were a key to her understanding of why she should do this. They enabled Christina to realize the need to "lend a helping hand."

Carly Jackson, the other co-president of the North Hollywood High School VAMS group with Christina, agreed that being exposed to the trouble-ridden urban environment of the part of Los Angeles where she lived and went to school influenced her to engage in civic work. A combination of particularly disturbing events also convinced her that she should do what she could to help those in need in her community.

Yet it would be inaccurate to conclude that negative factors like those that Christina, Carly, and I experienced are the sole reasons why we and other young people engage in civic work. Exposure to community service, whether through a youth organization, academic courses, or parents and family, can be crucial, as I learned from Carly and other student volunteers like Michelle Florentine and Roxanne Heston. These students were among those who impressed me as especially dedicated volunteers when I founded VAMS at North Hollywood High School. When I began working with them, I immediately noticed their glowing passion and motivation for helping others. Revisiting them two years after I graduated from high school, I found that their dedication for serving others had not only continued, but also developed and deepened. Public service was an integral part of their lives, and they had assumed leadership roles in the North Hollywood VAMS group. VAMS was an important, but certainly not the sole factor in their decision to serve others. They had all begun journeys in public service as young children.

Girl Scouts influenced Carly Jackson's decision to devote time to public service. Joining the program in the first grade and continuing it until the eighth grade, Carly was exposed to community-service projects at an early age, and the leadership activities of Girl Scouts influenced her to continue civic work in high school. She sewed fleece caps for cancer patients shortly after she learned how to thread a needle, volunteered at soup kitchens just as she was discovering how to flip an omelet, and organized bake sale fundraisers when mastering arithmetic. In the third grade, Carly and other girls in Troop 652 attended an event to celebrate the holiday season at a school run by Para Los Niños, a nonprofit that serviced disadvantaged children in the Los Angeles and San Bernardino counties.

All the members of Troop 653 donned sparkly brown reindeer ears and the symbolic Girl Scout uniforms covered with badges acquired over the years of their membership. They were then introduced to foster-care children, and each Girl Scout was assigned a child for whom to purchase a gift. Carly presented a shiny striped gift box. As ribbon unraveled and gift-wrap paper was tossed aside, colorful blobs of Play-dough quickly transformed into funny-looking animals. The two girls sat around poking and pounding the modeling clay, and playing together. "It seemed like the normal thing to do," reminisced Carly. She shared with me that when you are younger, you often do not need to understand the tough realities of why you should give back to community: you just go in and play with the kids in need. Carly later entered high school with the assumption that people *should* be doing public service, and that she herself had to continue her community involvement.

Although not actively involved in a youth service organization like Girl Scouts, Roxanne Heston took a service-learning course offered by the Center for Talented Youth before joining VAMS in high school. The course, which was for gifted youth, consisted of visiting and learning about the derelict parts of Baltimore, where shops lacked shimmering signs, and sidewalks consisted of grass-penetrated terrains of broken concrete. These field trips enlightened Roxanne and drove her desire to help other people.

One of the first outings, Roxanne told me, was to a homeless shelter. She and her classmates had walked across the city of Baltimore, passing tall, majestic skyscrapers and long, clear glass walls, until they finally reached a set of dismal, flat buildings. They had arrived at the shelter, a grimy shanty decked with homemade posters and packed with a mix of homeless people. A paunchy woman grinned with her assortment of colored teeth. Someone cloaked in an oversized coat muttered to no one in particular while shifting his weight in the corner. "We had to turn our heads to keep from staring," Roxanne said as she thought with a shudder of the images that had surrounded her. But once she and her classmates began touring the shelter, they were almost forced to engage in conversations with its residents. During this time, the students soon realized that the anonymous homeless women surrounding them had names, including Lois and Helena, and with those names came complex personalities.

Lois, Helena, and the other shelter occupants began discussing with the students favorite meals at McDonalds, celebrity gossip, and television shows. Time quickly elapsed and upon leaving the shelter, Roxanne had what she describes as "a simple revelation": "homeless" is merely a title for people without a home, a title that does not imply that they never had a home, do not have a job or friends, or do not exhibit every other quality that so called "normal" people do. Homeless people are people too, and they can have pasts and interests similar to our own. This awareness and comparable insights from other field trips that Roxanne took with the Center for Talented Youth encouraged her to continue to engage in civic work.

Michelle Florentine, whom I also met through VAMS, had a similar realization during her childhood. Although she did not participate in a youth service organization as Carly did, or an academic course as Roxanne did, Michelle's mother was a pathologist and regular volunteer for the American Cancer Society. One's familial upbringing is critical to character development. Tom had parents who were committed to civic work, and likewise, Michelle's family outings consisted of running marathons through streets lined with pink ribbons for breast cancer awareness and donning white medical coats to assist at hospital pathology centers.

One place Michelle's family regularly visited was Henry Mayo Newhall Memorial Hospital. Every year, the Hospital held an event for the teenage girls of Valencia High School at which they could learn the dangers of smoking. Michelle's mother usually led the event and her entire family would assist in finding and bringing in photos of lung cells destroyed by smoking.

"This is a normal lung," twelve-year-old Michelle would explain to girls who were often older than she was. "This is a cancerous lung. Don't smoke, or your lung will turn into this." Michelle and her siblings began attending the conferences as bystanders, observing their mother as she educated people about cancer, but they soon began to staff the information stations and educate others as they grew older.

Michelle's involvement in cancer awareness continued in high school when she gathered signatures for a proposition to raise the tax on cigarettes. "Doing community service at a young age helped make it clear that I should continue it in high school," Michelle told me, mirroring Carly's sentiments.

My conversations with these three dedicated high school VAMS volunteers, served to make me realize that the nonprofit I had created was certainly not the sole factor in encouraging them to assist others. Growing up exposed to opportunities for service at an early age helped these individuals realize the need to help other people in the world. VAMS was simply a stepping-stone opportunity for them proactively to reach out with other extremely passionate youth. At the same time, I know that there were almost certainly other motives that Carly, Roxanne, Michelle, and other volunteers did not share with me.

My high school had a local chapter of California Scholarship Federation (CSF), an honors society that required strong academic standing and a certain number of community service hours each semester. Many students in the Highly Gifted Magnet program wanted to be a part of CSF, and performing enough service hours while consistently maintaining good grades semester after semester allowed students to become "life members", with a fancy lamp pin, nice tassels at graduation, and an extra gold seal on their high-school diplomas. Unlike many of the other student-organized community service clubs on campus, I had registered VAMS with the IRS as a 501(c)(3) nonprofit organization. As such, the community-service coordinator for CSF allowed me to sign off on my peers' volunteer hours for CSF.

I did not abuse this role by allocating more hours than volunteers deserved—moral leadership is another lesson of this book—but I do feel a bit guilty that I found this responsibility to be a particularly effective way to attract volunteers. "Sure, you can satisfy your community service requirements through VAMS," I remember my friends and I would tell our classmates. "It's a lot more fun than volunteering by yourself."

As we did this, my leadership team and I would awkwardly stare down at the dark blobs of dried up gum that had accumulated on the floors outside the school cafeteria. Perhaps we realized that this approach didn't seem the most appropriate way to recruit volunteers, although it did work well. I would like to think that all the volunteers we had were not simply driven by self-serving motives like lifetime membership in an honor society. I would like to think that most of them had altruistic motives like the ones Christina, Carly, and Roxanne described. But I know that motives are mixed.

LESSON 5

Moral Leadership Is Essential in Civic Work

TOM AND ERNESTINE

Our headlines are often crowded with stories of civic leaders who stumble morally when doing their civic work, and even more often with tales of civic leaders whose personal lives are morally flawed. We think the connection between personal and public morality is not as clear-cut as many news commentators would suggest. But we do recognize that civic leaders, whether in charge of nonprofit organizations or government agencies, should be role models, particularly for those people who work with them, and moral lapses in their personal lives often leave scars that weaken their moral authority in their professional capacities.

However one views the impact of private immorality by those doing civic work, there can be no question that moral rectitude in civic work is an essential component of civic leadership. A few lines from *The Duke's Children* by one of Tom's favorite novelists, Anthony Trollope, capture what we have in mind. The Duke, who had been Prime Minister of England, is writing to his son, newly elected to Parliament:

> ...always remember the purpose for which there is a Parliament elected... It is not that some men may shine there, that some may acquire power, or that all may plume themselves on being the elect of the nation... A member of Parliament should feel himself to be the servant of his country,—and like every other servant, he should

serve... You are there as the guardian of your fellow-countrymen,—
that they may be safe, that they may be prosperous, that they may be
well governed and lightly burdened,—above all that they may be
free. (*The World's Classics*. Oxford University Press, 1951. 148-49.)

Both of us have faced issues of moral leadership in our civic work, as we
discuss in the pages that follow. Ernestine describes the elements of
that leadership: selflessness, genuineness, integrity, and empathy. And
she illustrates each of the elements with stories that demonstrate these
qualities through the actions of young civic leaders. Tom also recounts
the essential nature of moral leadership in civic leaders with whom he
has worked, using examples from his experiences in public service to
illustrate this Lesson.

TOM

In my first administrative role, as dean of Stanford Law School, I had
responsibility for looking some years into the future and trying to determine what would be the roles and responsibilities of lawyers. As I began
to learn the extent to which lawyers served and did not serve the legal
needs of Americans, I became increasingly aware that most poor people
were deprived of legal services when they most needed those services
because they could not afford to pay the costs. Learned Hand, speaking
at the 75th Anniversary Dinner of the New York Legal Aid Society,
concluded his extemporaneous remarks with this aphorism, "If we are
to keep our democracy strong, there must be one commandment: Thou
shalt not ration justice." Over time, I became deeply troubled by the
harsh reality that justice was rationed in America.

I had a chance to help deal with this problem after I had served five
years as dean at Stanford Law School and had accomplished my major
goals. The first capital campaign in the School's history was successfully
concluded, with the funds raised for a completely new set of buildings,
for endowed professorships, and for student scholarships. A major overhaul of the curriculum, organized by a committee that I chaired before
I became dean, was working well. The School had hired its first female
and first Black faculty members, which may seem hard to believe now
since this was less than forty years ago. A number of other leading law

scholars had joined the faculty. The School had taken other important—though less visible—steps as well.

Therefore, when I learned that a new public corporation had been established by Congress to take nation-wide responsibility for the provision of legal services to poor people, I wanted the job of leading that new entity, called the Legal Services Corporation. Ellen was skeptical of leaving California and returning to Washington, though we knew that we would keep our house in Palo Alto and would one day return. But she agreed that this could be a wonderful position for me and that I should apply. Having never worked in legal services for the poor, I was initially concerned that this would be a disabling liability. As it happened, the politics of the appointment process among the Corporation's Board of Directors was such that my inexperience proved to be an advantage for me.

The Legal Services Corporation took over a program that was started as part of President Johnson's "War Against Poverty" and was run out of the Office of Economic Opportunity in the White House. It was one of a number of programs designed to help poor people, and it was one of the most successful. But because it was responsible for lawsuits against financially powerful interests, it was also one of the most controversial. When Richard Nixon became president, his Vice President, Spiro Agnew, started an aggressive campaign to abolish the legal-services program. In response, supporters of the program in Congress proposed that federally-funded legal services be run by a public corporation, responsible directly to Congress and not part of the Executive Branch.

In the last days of the Nixon administration, when he was fighting the looming prospect of impeachment, he agreed to support legislation to create the Legal Services Corporation, thinking this would help him gain favor with some Democrats. The ploy failed, of course, and Gerald Ford became president. But the legislation was adopted. It took a long time, however, before the Senate finally confirmed a Board of Directors. The Congressional Act that established the Corporation required that half of the Board be Democrats and half Republicans. President Ford followed the statute in a literal sense, but all of his proposed appointees were extreme conservatives, and the Senate refused to confirm most of them. Months passed before a compromise was reached between the Democratic majority in the Senate and the White House, and the eleven-person Board was finally confirmed.

The new Board represented a range of perspectives, but a majority were conservatives who nonetheless believed that poor people deserved representation by a lawyer when they were faced with critical issues that involved the law. This majority wanted someone as the first president who would represent a break with the Office of Economic Opportunity past. During the time of that Office, federally funded legal services had grown under President Johnson, but funding had been frozen at $74 million for the previous five years under President Nixon. This funding was supposed to pay for legal services to more than thirty million people living below the federally-established poverty line. In this period, the local programs supported with federal legal-services monies were concentrated largely in urban areas along the east and west coasts, for those were the areas where bar and other local groups were most receptive. As a result, many sections of the Midwest, the South, and the Southwest were totally without any legal help for poor people except through the voluntary efforts of private attorneys.

The Board of the Corporation included a former Stanford Law School professor named Sam Thurman, who was at the time dean of the University of Utah Law School and a friend of mine. When I heard that the Board had finally been confirmed and was looking for a president, I called Sam and told him of my interest. He said that given all the problems facing the new entity, he was not sure he understood why I wanted the job, but that he would be glad to support me. Sam was respected by everyone on the Board as a wise moderate, and his support was one of the two fortunate breaks I had on the way to being chosen. The second was that the chair of the Board, Roger Crampton, was then the dean of Cornell Law School. He had formerly been in the Nixon Justice Department as head of the Office of Legal Counsel, but resigned well before the Watergate crisis. Roger was a thoughtful conservative and a person of great personal integrity. We knew each other, though not well. When he heard that I was being nominated, and that Sam Thurman was supportive, he immediately backed my candidacy. Others on the Board, no doubt, were impressed by the reputation of Stanford. In all events, over the course of the late fall I had a series of interviews with the Board search committee and was offered the position, which I accepted effective January 1, 1976.

During the Nixon years, not only was federal funding for legal services frozen, but for all that period, until he was forced to resign, Vice President Agnew had focused an ugly verbal attack on the program, arguing that taxpayers should not be supporting a program that sponsored private-party suits against landlords, local merchants, and others. The fact that judges were deciding in favor of poor people in the overwhelming share of these cases only made Agnew angrier and his abuse even shriller.

As a result, I knew that the lawyers and paralegals working in local programs felt beaten down and dispirited. I also knew that these public officials wanted as Legal Services Corporation president someone who had worked in the "trenches" of legal services over the past five years. As an outsider, they would naturally view me with some suspicion. I realized that I needed to appoint as my deputy a person who would immediately be seen by this group as "one of them." Fortunately, a dear friend of mine fit that bill perfectly: Clint Bamberger, the former dean of the Law School at the Catholic University of America. Previously, he had served in the Office of Economic Opportunity as the head of the federal legal-services program. Clint and I had become friends while we were fellow deans, and when he left that role I had invited him to spend a semester at Stanford where our friendship grew even closer.

When I was being considered as president, Roger Crampton made clear that if I were chosen, all hiring would be under my sole control, and he had cleared this stance with all members of the Board. As soon as I received word that I had been chosen, I called Clint and offered him the role of executive vice president. "I want you to be my alter ego," I told him. I knew that I would necessarily be particularly focused on dealing with the Board, with Congress, and with creating public support for the program. He would, I said, be primarily concerned with program operations and internal issues. To my great relief, Clint told me immediately and enthusiastically that he would be pleased to accept my offer.

Clint and I soon set about planning what would be needed for the Legal Services Corporation. The Board was set to vote on our appointments at its meeting in early January. This would be just a formality, since Crampton had talked with the Board members who were not on the search committee, and he told me they were all enthusiastic about my appointment and understood that I would be responsible for all hiring.

Crampton suggested that we organize a reception to occur right after the January Board meeting and that we invite a large group of legal-services people, Congressional members and their staffs, and others who might be helpful to the Corporation. I would be sworn in as the new president and Bamberger as the Executive Vice President. Afterwards, Board members, Bamberger, and I would all have a chance to mingle with the guests at the reception.

With help from those in legal services, Clint and I put together a guest list, and were delighted when over 500 people agreed to come to the reception in a downtown Washington hotel. I had asked U.S. Supreme Court Justice Byron White to swear me into office. He and I had become good friends when our families and we were together for a month at the Salzburg Seminar in Austria, where he and I were both lecturing.

In the week before the Board meeting, a conservative columnist, James J. Kirkpatrik, wrote an angry column that was printed in hundreds of newspapers. In the column, he bemoaned the fact that I had been chosen — a liberal Democrat, who had worked in the Kennedy and Johnson administrations. But much, much worse, he wrote, was the selection of Bamberger as executive vice president, for Bamberger was "pink." He had misdirected the Office of Economic Opportunity legal-services office, and he would be a disastrous leader of the new federal effort.

The Board, meeting in the hotel where the reception was scheduled, began with a luncheon, which included both Bamberger and me, and 10 of the 11 Board members. The eleventh, Judge Revius Ortique from New Orleans, the only Black appointee, was delayed getting to Washington. Then about 1:00 p.m., Bamberger and I were asked to leave the Board meeting while the Board briefly discussed and then voted on our appointments. Under the statute establishing the Corporation, Board approval was required for both of us, but Crampton had assured me that this was just a formality. So Bamberger and I left the meeting room and moved to a large area next door where the reception would be held.

About 2:00 p.m. Crampton came out, ashen faced, and asked me to join him in a small room adjacent to where he had been having lunch with the rest of the Board. When he closed the door he told me that at least half of the Board wanted me to withdraw the name of Bamberger as "too divisive." I would be approved, they said, but only if I withdrew the nomination of Bamberger. In effect, Crampton reported, these Board members wanted a clean start for the Corporation and this would not be possible with Bamberger in a leadership position. I later learned that the Kirkpatrik column was the key to this hard-line stand.

I had to make a decision about how to respond, and in retrospect it was one of the morally critical moments in my professional life. I did not hesitate for an instant in telling Crampton that I could not serve as president without Bamberger as my partner. I had asked Bamberger to join me, I said, and having done so I could not go back on my personal commitment. I said I had a moral obligation to keep that commitment. I also said that I could do the job at the standard I thought necessary only with Bamberger as my colleague. To his great credit, Crampton said, "I thought you would say that, and I will support you and do everything I can to ensure that you are both approved." He then went back in the luncheon room and I returned to sit with Bamberger.

In retrospect, I realize that I answered without considering a lot of problems that would arise if the Board decided to hold firm about Bamberger. Ellen and I had made plans to move to Washington, though she would not be joining me with two of our children until school was out in the summer. I had resigned as dean at Stanford Law School and a search was under way for a new dean, so I could not return to that position, though I could go back as a professor there. The Legal Services Corporation, having struggled for well over a year to get started, would be without leadership for much longer while a new search was organized. It would no doubt be known what had happened, so finding a new leader would not be easy. And so forth. But I frankly considered none of these as critically important matters—only my moral obligation to Bamberger and to my word.

I came back to the reception room and told Bamberger what had happened. He immediately offered to withdraw his name. But I told him that he was exactly the right person for the Corporation and for me, and that the Corporation would either be led by both of us or by neither of us.

Time passed as Bamberger and I sat in the reception room surrounded by mounds of food. About 3:00 p.m., I called Justice White and said that he should not come to swear me into office. Bamberger and I then made lists of close friends who were coming. We called them between 3:30 and 4:00 p.m., explained what happened, and gave each a list of other people to call to say the reception was cancelled, but not to say why. We thought the news would get out soon enough, and there was no need to cause further agitation. At 5:00 p.m., Crampton came out to say that the Board was still talking, but that it was now split 5 to 5. Revius Ortique was expected, but not until late that night. Bamberger and I went to his house for dinner and a long wait. Finally, I received a call from Crampton at 11:00 p.m. to say that Ortique had arrived at the meeting, had voted for both of us, and that we would be sworn in at a Board meeting the next morning.

Bamberger and I arrived together the next morning, not being quite sure what to expect. The Board voted to confirm us, six to five, and I might have expected that our leadership would have been severely handicapped in our new roles, particularly in dealing with the minority of the Board who have been against Bamberger. But this was the last serious conflict I had with the Board. All the members apparently decided that they should put that issue behind them. Ironically, having gotten off to such a rocky start, the Board was unanimous in supporting me during a series of very controversial steps Bamberger and I took in the next three years.

This was not, of course, the first time that I have felt the importance of following my moral conscious. But it was the first time when I had to make a career-determining decision based on my moral judgment. As I have reflected on that decision, I have come to believe that those doing civic work have a particular obligation to chart the moral path and to follow it to an even greater degree than those in the private sector because they are privileged to work with public funds and public trust.

My core "test" of an action or inaction is whether I would be comfortable in having it appear on the front page of a major newspaper. I do not know who first suggested this approach, which I have appropriated, but it seems right for me because it forces me to be sure that I can defend responsibly, with a clear conscience, the decision I am making. While I cannot claim to have followed the approach at all times, I have tried and found it usually provides a sound basis for judgment. Although I did not invent this approach, I found it imprinted on my psyche soon after I became president of the Legal Services Corporation. I took a very significant compensation cut when I left the Stanford

Law School deanship for this position, and the Board of the Corporation wanted to help me in every way it could, while following the statute that established the Corporation and also set my salary. So the Board proposed that I have the free use of a modest-sized car, which would be helpful for me in driving to and from work and to visit legal-services offices, but could also be used for my own purposes. One day I found a front-page article in the *Washington Post*, criticizing the Board for authorizing the car and me for accepting its use. The head of a program to help poor people should not, the article suggested, have the free use of a car. On reflection, I continued to believe that the car was a reasonable benefit for me to have, but my "test" was highlighted in my mind forever afterward.

It was my good fortune to come to my "cross-roads" decision at the Legal Services Corporation after I had been mentored by moral leaders in civic work who showed me by their examples the power and importance of moral decision making. These are a few illustrations that stand out in my mind.

When I was a young assistant to Abram Chayes, Legal Adviser in the State Department, I was assigned the role of legal counsel for the State Department in negotiating the sale of nuclear missiles to the United Kingdom, which had been agreed to by President Kennedy and British Prime Minister MacMillan. This was the first sale of nuclear missiles to any foreign government and the negotiations at the Pentagon were cloaked in great secrecy. The U.S. negotiating team was headed by a full admiral, who was assisted by numerous other Defense Department officials, including someone from the General Counsel's office, and by various State Department officials. We met over the course of several days.

At the outset, the admiral in charge of the U.S. team said, in effect, "Let's agree that no transcript will be kept of the negotiations so that no one will feel inhibited about speaking. In short, there will be no records kept until we have the final text of an agreement covering all aspects of the sale." The British agreed and the negotiations proceeded. At the end of the second day of negotiations, everyone else had left the room where we were meeting in the Pentagon, and I was alone there when a sailor came in, ducked under the table around which we had all been sitting, and pulled out a box from which he extracted several recording tapes. It was instantly clear to me that a secret recording machine had been recording all our discussions. I quickly went to the Defense Department lawyer who had been present and told him that the recording violated the commitment not to keep a record of the proceedings. "Oh, don't worry about that," he told me. "The British will never know."

But I did worry about it, and when I returned to the State Department I told this story to Chayes. He immediately called Rusk and asked for an appointment urgently. A few minutes later we went up to the Secretary's cavernous office on the seventh floor, where I repeated my tale to Rusk. While Chayes and I were still in his office, Rusk picked up a special phone that connected him directly to Secretary of Defense McNamara. Rusk told McNamara my story and said it was not acceptable for the United States to be violating its word to our closest ally. McNamara did not wait to hear his colleagues' side of the story, but instantly agreed that the recording would be suspended.

The moral leadership that both Rusk and McNamara exhibited made a deep impression on me. Rusk, incidentally, thanked me with the following story. He was a young foreign service officer when George Marshal was Secretary of State soon after the end of World War II. One day Rusk did something that Marshall thought was particularly significant. "You earned your pay, today," Rusk was told by Marshall. And Rusk turned to me and said, "Tom, you earned your pay today." Though I came to believe deeply that George W. Ball was right about the need for the United States to take its troops out of Vietnam, and that Dean Rusk was profoundly wrong on that issue, Rusk always impressed me in terms of his personal integrity and moral leadership.

The next year, when I was working for George W. Ball, we were grappling with an explosive and extremely difficult crisis in Cyprus. Though the island is small, its strategic location was critical because of British military bases located there. Archbishop Makarios was the president of the Government, and a constant thorn in the side of the United States. He delighted in verbal attacks on the United States and in threats to limit our ability to use Cyprus for our defensive purposes.

I often sat in on intelligence briefings for Ball and Rusk by members of what was termed "the intelligence community." At one of these meetings, with representatives present from the CIA, the Defense Department, the National Security Agency, and the State Department—and chaired by Ball—someone from the CIA said, "Well, you know, it might not be so difficult to ensure that Archbishop Makarios is assassinated." He went on to suggest that this could be done in such a way that there would "be no U.S. fingerprints." George W. Ball was a big man, about 6'4" tall and weighing well over 200 pounds. He reared back in his chair and in a voice that totally dominated the room announced, "The United States of America and its Government does not do assassinations."

Later Ball told me that he thought the State Department had implicitly authorized the South Vietnamese military coup in which president Diem was assassinated, and he felt that he personally should have found a way to stop it. Whether or not Ball could have done so, I am quite clear that if he had said in the meeting I attended, perhaps with a wink and a nod, that it would be convenient to have Markarios out of the way, those in the CIA would have successfully found a means to make that happen. The moral lesson stuck with me.

I do not suggest that moral leadership in public service need necessarily involve such important issues. To the contrary, the matters more often are much more modest in consequence, though following conscience is always involved. On rare occasions, that may even mean doing something the law does not allow. A small incident in my early life as a lawyer struck home this point to me. I was in my first month as a new lawyer at the firm of Foley & Lardner in Milwaukee. The firm was particularly attractive to me because I was promised an opportunity to work in a wide range of different fields in a short period of time. One of my first assignments was to meet with a client of the firm, a couple, who wanted to set up a new corporation. I knew that this was no more complicated than typing in the name of the new corporation on a form supplied by the Wisconsin Secretary of State, listing the corporate officers on the form, and then filing it with the Secretary of State's Office. I ushered the couple into a conference room, listened while they told me that they wanted themselves to be the president and secretary of the corporation, and to list their names on the form. "I will be delighted to do that Mr. and Mrs. Smith," I said with some pride, and when they were gone I proceeded to instruct a secretary to list Mr. Smith as president and Mrs. Smith as secretary, as they had asked me to do. I then sent the form off to the Secretary of State for filing. I had just completed my first solo task as a lawyer and was feeling overly proud of myself.

A few weeks later, I was filling out an internal law-firm form to explain how my time should be charged and I saw a notation for "Mr. and Mrs. Smyth: formation of new corporation." I suddenly realized, of course, that I had misspelled what I thought was the simplest surname. And I had in my desk, waiting for the couple to come into my office again, a certificate of incorporation with the wrong spelling. The only way to change this under Wisconsin law was for the couple to sign a form asking for an amendment of the certificate. For this to occur, of course, would mean that they would know exactly what had happened.

I was in a total panic, and can still feel the sweat rising on my face. After an agonized hour, I picked up the phone and called the Wisconsin Secretary of State. Given the prestige of my law firm, he answered the phone without delay, though I had never met him. I confessed exactly what had happened. After a long silence, during which I was increasingly uncomfortable, the Secretary of State finally said, "Why don't you come up here this afternoon with the certificate, and we will see what we can do." I drove from Milwaukee to Madison, and came to his office. When I was ushered in, he closed the door and asked me to give him the certificate of incorporation. He handed me back a new one with the names of the officers and incorporators properly spelled. He did not have to inform me that what he had done was quite beyond his legal authority. Perhaps I only delude myself to think he did not only a charitable act of great kindness, but also a moral one. At the least, I hope this is true. In all events, during subsequent years, I have often thought of this incident when I have been in positions of authority and subordinates have made mistakes through lack of care and attention. I hope I have followed his example.

ERNESTINE

Losses, failures, and mistakes splashed the headlines of the *Stanford Daily* and *Stanford Review*, criticizing our student government. A room in Old Union decorated with soft body pillows, plushy beanbags, and colorful finger paintings had been called the Wellness Room. It was a student-government project under Student Services Division and intended to promote healthy living by providing a place for relaxation on campus. But in reality, many students condemned the Wellness Room as simply being like a children's playroom. Perhaps even worse was the Shuttle Service. It was created to provide affordable transportation for students traveling back and forth from campus to the airport. But it was criticized for its continuous financial loss and lack of ability to cater to the entire student body. During my freshman year, for example, the winter-break shuttles had cost student government about $13,000 but only about $11,000 was made in revenue. Essentially, student government was subsidizing the cost of rides home for only a limited number students, and this caused the program to be highly criticized, especially as student-government funds were aggregated from general student fees that *all* students at Stanford contributed to. The *Stanford Daily* quoted various members of the Undergraduate Senate who noted "the tremendously wasteful nature of the program," and some even expressed "doubt that the ASSU shuttle bus program will be renewed." Many undergraduate students debated extensively on the merits of the program.

Wellness Room and Shuttle Service were two of many service programs that were all a part of Student Services Division (SSD), then one of the four main branches of student government. SSD oversaw student-initiated programs and projects within student government. Debates about these two programs soon turned into debates on the virtues of SSD itself. Undergraduate senators debated whether it was even worth providing the director with a stipend, whether other programs within SSD such as Tutoring for Community should be cut from funding, and in extreme cases, whether SSD was even worth the energy. When I joined SSD near the end of my freshman year, it was simply a mess, to say the very least.

Reviving a "failed," dying organization is far from easy. I was hired as deputy director of SSD, while a senior classmate, Elaine Albertson, was the executive director. I had been involved in student government throughout my freshman year, and several student leaders thought Elaine and I would work well together to revive the organization.

Elaine was a delight to work with. She would always bring treats to our meetings as we called potential partner companies to compare shuttle costs and services, created a marketing plan, recruited freshman interns to assist us, and worked together to turn around the Shuttle Service. We met with our interns every other day, student leaders every week, and the director of the Haas Center for Public Service every month. Over many months, we poured in hours working at Old Union, where the student-government offices were located. We shaped projects focused on arts and entertainment such as Stanford Concert Network, education such as Student Initiated Courses, event-planning resources such as Old Union Room Reservations, sustainability programs such as Green Store, and several other services. In short, I probably spent more time with Elaine than with any textbook for any class I had at Stanford.

Then December hit. Elaine concluded she needed to focus on academics, her honors thesis, and starting a master's program. She decided to step down as the executive director, and I was promoted. I was then only a sophomore in college, and unsure if I could handle the responsibility of managing an organization with thousands of dollars in assets. Fortunately, Elaine remained involved, and I quickly realized that moral leadership is about having a vested interest in the organization you are leading. This interest can come in many forms—staying on board to see a project come to fruition, ensuring a smooth transition in leadership, and making sure the organization is still able to continue and thrive, even if and when you step down.

Elaine remained involved in SSD, ensuring a smooth transition and continuing to work with me throughout the following year as the freshmen internship director. I am proud to say that the Shuttle Service ran profitably that year for the first time ever, and our proposed budget passed with no pushback from the student body. Later, I was able to hire Patrick Lee and Eileen Ung—both individuals I thought also displayed qualities of moral leaders—to succeed me.

Over time, I have begun to realize that true civic leaders are moral leaders. What do I mean by moral leadership? There are many elements, but in my view the key dimensions are selflessness, genuineness, integrity, and empathy. Civic volunteers of all ages taught me the meaning and importance of these core traits.

Eileen Ung's dimples are quite contagious. Quick to smile, Eileen encourages others around her to light up as well. She's attentive to opportunities to help, does nice things for people she doesn't know, and practices three acts of kindness for every blessing she receives. She is selfless when she both takes and gives.

Chatting with Eileen, I was reminded of days when I felt pure euphoria going to the library, first in the summer when the building served as a convenient escape from the blazing heat outside, and then later to participate in after-school programs. There was the special thrill of grabbing a worn book or magazine, passing it to a young volunteer reader, and plopping into a pile of giant stuffed animals in the children's corner of the library. When Eileen visited her local public library in elementary school, she participated in an after-school program where she not only experienced the comforting moments of someone reading a story aloud, but also received free tutoring on her schoolwork.

Walking past the metal security bars on the library doors, into a blast of cooling air conditioning, Eileen would first meander to the back of the library, past shelves and shelves of books and plush sofas. School had just ended for the day, and homework was not the first thing she wanted to do. Casually grabbing a magazine and flipping through colorful pages filled with everything from beauty tips to the latest celebrity gossip, Eileen would squander some time before recalling that the tutoring center closed at 5:00 p.m., and she had homework to do. Scrambling across the library to a simple room tucked away on the side, Eileen saw the all-too-familiar round table with three chairs and a couple of computers scattered behind it. This—Dana Library's Family Tutoring Center—had become Eileen's second home. She used the computers here because the ones her family owned did not have Internet access, and dozens of college students had volunteered their time to help her with homework here. Geometry, specifically angles, was Eileen's Achilles heel. It was that last math problem in her geometry homework that Eileen always struggled with, the one on the last page of her assignment, dotted with an asterisk to highlight its difficulty. Eileen would sit with a tutor, usually Josh, and work through, step by step, how to solve the problem.

Things changed in middle school. Eileen would return to the library daily, but this time, to enter a different room, now giving rather than receiving help. "I want to tutor others because tutoring helped me for so long," Eileen told me. "The person in front of me needs help. I can assist her and others like her." This became her new mantra. At an early age, Eileen recognized the wisdom of paying it forward: when someone helps you, do not just thank him or her. Repay the person by performing an act of kindness to someone else. Or three acts of kindness. Or many more. Acts of kindness are not something to do only when performing public service. Always try to make someone smile and encourage others to keep the ripple going.

This idea of selflessly giving to others—selflessness—is part of a larger picture of moral leadership in civic work. Another part is a sense of genuineness, a trait ingrained in the character of Garrett Neiman. As Garrett taught me, public service should not be a casual, one-time activity, but rather a journey you should begin once you are conscious of the world around you, up until the time you die. To meet Garrett is to encounter someone that is genuine in all aspects of his life, including his dedication to civic work. Upon graduating from Stanford, Garrett turned a student-led service project into an organization that helps transform the lives of at-risk children. Garrett is a genuine public-service leader, a moral leader.

Garrett's story is one of many I have heard, but it can well serve to underscore this key virtue of genuineness, which is evident on meeting him. He had learned as a Stanford undergraduate that most low-income students had no chance to take a SAT preparatory course. Garrett had the insight that the test scores of these students were often several hundred points lower than they might have been with good coaching. Instead of simply muttering to himself that the whole system needed revamping, that life is too often unfair, and so forth, Garrett went out and did something to change the chances of many of these high-school graduates to go to college. He started CollegeSpring, with a particular focus on students in East Palo Alto, a very poor community. He developed a manual for preparing students who did not have the benefit of programs such as the Princeton Review or Kaplan. He enlisted Stanford students to help as unpaid volunteers over the summer. From the start, the results of his efforts were remarkable. Average test scores of students in his program were nearly two hundred points higher than the scores of similar students not in the program, and students were also prepared for the college admissions and financial-aid process.

Garrett wanted to do more to promote and expand CollegeSpring, but he was torn. As he told me his story, it was fall quarter of his final year at Stanford. Bright summer flip-flops, neon frisbees, and clusters of students tanning on Wilbur Field were gradually disappearing. Leaves covered the rooftops of cars, sidewalks, and the overhangs of buildings. These events all signified an important time for many students at Stanford, particularly the seniors—a slew of job offers, and rejections, were flowing in, and there was the anticipation of graduation and having to trudge out into the work world.

Garrett had received an offer from McKinsey and Company, a top global consulting firm, an offer for which many of his peers yearned. "It's one of the most prestigious firms in the industry," Garrett told himself with pride. "Its platform and reputation will be extremely valuable to me." With that attitude, he accepted the McKinsey offer for January of the following year, which left him seven months to wrap up a few projects before beginning work full-time.

One of many things Garrett planned to do was to spend some time with an individual who later became an anonymous donor to CollegeSpring. An immigrant from China, this person felt lucky to have attended UC Berkeley and Stanford. He became an extraordinarily successful businessman, and he felt that the access to higher education provided him with the resources he needed to launch a career in investment banking and entrepreneurship. The man wanted to help organizations that were working hard to connect more students to top universities. CollegeSpring, the nonprofit Garrett founded to provide free SAT preparation and college counseling services to low-income students, was just such an organization.

Sitting across from the man at a coffee shop in downtown Palo Alto, Garrett recalled the man's offer to donate $250,000 if Garrett could raise an equal amount so that CollegeSpring could merge with a similar group on the east coast. As Garrett shared this incident with me, I imagine the conversation went something along the lines of the following. "I want to see CollegeSpring (then called SEE College Prep) continue to make an impact," the man said. "I think you can outgrow the organization you're planning to merge with." Those words frequently resurfaced in Garrett's mind as the conversation continued, and he began to focus on the idea of working full-time to expand CollegeSpring. "If I turn down McKinsey," Garrett began, nervously toying with the napkin dispenser in front of him, "Will you fund my nonprofit for the next two years?" "How much?" the man responded. "Half a million dollars," Garrett replied. "It'll allow us to hire our initial team for two years."

The deal was done. "He made it happen," Garrett shared with me. "The amount of money he donated to CollegeSpring to become a full-time operation was key to our success." And this is true. But that donation would never have happened had Garrett not exhibited the key quality of genuineness in his own commitment to helping others.

The anonymous donor's landmark gift enabled Garrett to expand his work, and CollegeSpring became no longer merely a part-time commitment. While Garrett told me that he would not have worked full-time to build a nonprofit organization if he did not have the funds to do so, I doubt anything else was really an option for Garrett. He would have made it happen somehow. Garrett recognizes the importance of performing civic work as an integral part of his identity, a lifelong commitment to helping others. Moral leadership, as Garrett illustrates, is about being genuine, authentic in your commitment to civic work.

Being a public-service leader is not just about cofounding a nonprofit or making civic work your primary job though, as Blaine Chatman helped me realize. Blaine is not a well-known name or a prominent figure in public service, but he exemplifies the importance of integrity in civic leaders, the third of the core characteristics that are essential. When you meet him, you immediately sense that he is a person whom you can trust. When he agrees to provide a service for a nonprofit organization—as he often did for small community-service projects we were both involved in at Stanford—I never had to question whether the service would really get done. I knew that Blaine's word was a firm commitment and that he would not fail to provide what he had promised.

Harjus Birk is another moral leader I admire, one who embodies the fourth key dimension of civic leadership. Harjus' empathy enables him to gain the trust of others. Most of us can often be so focused on what seems important to ourselves that we forget sometimes about those around us, but Harjus is always both self-aware and mindful of others. One afternoon, we were at Ray's Grill in Palo Alto when he shared his experience at Delek Hospital, halfway around the world, where he had worked for a summer.

Tucked in the foothills of the Himalayas, Delek Hospital provides low-cost health care to Tibetan refugees and other impoverished people in Dharamsala, India. "We don't want to be demanding. We're grateful to be treated for free," was the attitude that silently pervaded the rooms, hallways, and corners of the hospital, slowly wreaking havoc throughout Delek Hospital. Those at the hospital were shy about voicing their pains. Many died of tuberculosis, having waited months before asking to be treated.

Since arriving at the hospital, Harjus had seen two such patients die. "It should not have happened," he told me. Harjus thought this infectious disease that threatened so many people had to have a cure. But as he walked into the hospital, Harjus only saw mountains around him; that is, barriers he had to climb. Passing a small deck where the patients washed their *pulu* cloth, he was reminded of his difference from these Tibetan refugees. The hospital patients wore a traditional gown of sheepskin, while as a Sikh from India, Harjus wore a turban; one barrier. Yet he was a human being like the people he sought to help. A bit of clothing could not exclude him.

Many times, Harjus felt like giving up. The refugees preferred to remain anonymous. They were not receptive to outsiders, and even when they seemed to want help, the language barriers made communication difficult. Harjus could easily have taken the attitude that they should be grateful for his treatment, simply treating patients as people in need of his help. But to truly assist the patients, he knew he had to change the hospital's culture. That became his mission for the summer.

With a worn metal chair pulled up to the hospital bed, Harjus sat beside a Tibetan refugee. Harjus' hands were pressed together, his chin pointed down, and his eyes fixed on a small stain on the floor. He listened intently as the nurse translated the patient's tale, sentence by sentence, word by word. The story that Harjus heard was chilling.

"They often seized me from my family and forced me into a torture chamber. There I was attached to a wall, and forced to hang by my hands for hours at a time. This happened for over three years. I wanted to leave and run away, but I didn't want to leave my family," the refugee said.

Harjus finally had to look up. He could not bear seeing this elderly man, slouched across the hospital bed. "Do not use my name," the man interjected into his story. "I won't," Harjus responded, "I just want to listen."

"I finally realized I had to help myself," the man continued, "I had to escape. And now I am here. But I am not happy." He paused, tears trickling down a wrinkled cheek that had undergone too much darkness and sorrow. "I want to go back and save my family, even if I die."

Harjus heard bits of this story near the end of his summer internship. It was not a confidence the refugee would have shared earlier in the summer, when he barely knew Harjus, yet alone trusted him. But over time, Harjus was able to make the refugee feel understood, valued, and respected. Harjus' sensitivity towards others is one of the core traits that have made him a moral leader.

Without knowing Harjus, based on his external appearance, one might dismiss him as someone up to no good. The ragged scruffs and curls of his uncut beard, along with his maroon turban suggest that he is some sort of roguish foreigner. Mistaken for a Muslim, Harjus is often searched at the airport. Few recognize that his appearance is all part of his Sikh religion, which is intrinsic to his commitment to living an honest life.

Although I didn't know it at the time, Harjus had collaborated with Doctor Michael McCullough in his work at Delek Hospital, through McCullough's program BeAGoodDoctor.org. McCullough had introduced Harjus to the Delek Hospital, which he had become acquainted with while serving as the doctor to the Dalai Lama on some U.S. trips, and as an emergency-room physician in a center for the most serious types of trauma. Michael now serves on the board of the Dalai Lama Foundation and works with the Dalai Lama and Prime Minister of the Government in Exile, Lobsang Sangay, to provide leadership training for Tibetan youth.

Upon meeting Michael, I was reminded of Harjus, for both are moral leaders. Clothing and facial features are never Michael's concerns. Much too often, individuals prejudge the worth or value of someone by outward appearance alone. But Michael has a wonderful ability to see the inner person he is talking to or working with, and he pays no attention to the way that person is dressed. Upon meeting Michael, I recognized his empathy—a quality that cannot be developed over a short period of time. For Michael, the journey started at an early age, from the need to observe others. Michael had a brain hemorrhage at birth that was missed by the doctors, and as a result he subsequently suffered from hydrocephalus (water on the brain), that required life-saving brain surgery (a ventriculo-peritoneal shunt) when he was ten years old. Michael also had a severe stutter and other difficult coordination problems. He originally stuttered so severely that his twin brother Kevin often had to interpret his words to others for him. After his brain surgery he spent the next years retraining himself to speak, and made a special point of facing his fears directly.

On the fear front, even while he still stuttered, Michael took up stand-up comedy and later professional speaking. At the age of eighteen, he began winning public-speaking awards. In college, he founded the Stanford Medical Youth Science Program. Then in medical school and afterwards, Michael founded seven more nonprofits while working full-time as a medical doctor and entrepreneur. He is now a partner in a life-science investment fund, where his life experiences and wisdom have given him a fast footing in the venture industry. I have been fortunate to learn from him in ways that strengthen both my civic activities and my venture work, especially in terms of his abilities to empathize with those in need.

Michael would not call himself an eloquent speaker, even today, but the authenticity he gained from early childhood struggles allows him to carry a presence in his talks, despite the slight stutter which remains. His observation skills and empathy allow him to speak spontaneously for an hour or more about life strategy techniques, which he has done for students at Stanford, Princeton, and Yale, and received standing ovations.

Did Michael drastically change over those few years? Perhaps on the outside, it may seem so. But the roots of his remarkable strengths were planted in his early health struggles. By his own admission, he would not have been able to achieve so much were it not for the health and social hurdles he had to meet and overcome early in his life. Not being able to speak well until later in childhood promoted his observational skills and enabled him to look past the surface qualities of people to their core. I have met more than one student at Stanford who has worked with Michael or been mentored by him, and for many of those whom he takes under his wing, it has been a life-changing experience.

Looking back, it seemed somewhat natural that Michael would recruit Harjus. When moral leaders collaborate with one another, their efforts reinforce each other, as I realized with my colleagues at State Farm® Youth Advisory Board — some of the most remarkable young people I have met.

In public service, I have come to learn the fundamental rule that whenever possible you should work side-by-side with those whom you serve, rain or shine. Near the beginning of August, after my sophomore

year of college, a group of my contemporaries from around the country
spent a steaming summer day in Florida, working outside in humid,
100-degree weather for over eight hours. As either current or former
members of the State Farm® Youth Advisory Board, we wanted to feel
that we were not just handing out money, but really engaged in "sweat
labor" together for a civic project. Doing so could help us understand
just what our funding means to an organization in need. This was the
first time we were all gathered not to decide on which projects should
be funded by the Board, but rather to see first-hand the difference our
joint efforts could make in a community and to gain a clearer sense of
what kinds of projects could help young people bond through engaging
in a communal effort, as part of something larger than ourselves. We
decided to work with the Boys and Girls Club in Orlando, Florida, a
nonprofit that State Farm® had donated to multiple times. More important than the dollars involved, we wanted to inspire the youth members of the Club to engage in civic work and to develop the sense of
enthusiasm that has propelled each of us in our separate civic ventures.

When I walked outside, I noticed empty patches near the new play-
ground that had just been built a couple months ago. The Club members had not had the chance to improve the area yet, and we were eager
to help them to do so. Our goal was to plant trees around the recreation
area, make a sandpit for a volleyball court, and build a soccer field that
would include bleachers, backstops, and painted benches.

My primary task consisted of building a set of bleachers with a team
of about seven members of the Board and fifteen youth from the Boys
and Girls Club. Many of the youth we worked with had single-working
mothers and came from crime-filled neighborhoods. We arrived at the
center to greet them at eight in the morning, and then immediately set
to work moving sheets of metal and separating our materials into piles.
Over the next couple of hours, youth of different ages and spanning
different cultures poured over blueprints and slowly began constructing
the brace support frames. By noon, we were drilling holes and screwing
nuts to bolts. The heat and humidity were oppressive. At about 1:00
p.m., a supervisor stopped by to announce, "Lunch time! It's time to
eat!" No one budged. All of us were on our knees with sweat dripping
down our foreheads and arms and wrenches in our hands. One boy
even yelled back, "Five more minutes!" Everyone was so intent on the
work that food and air conditioning seemed trivial. It takes not only the

right types of people to make a civic organization succeed, but also a shared sense of mission and a common commitment to that mission. The right people surrounded me that day.

Several hours later, after finishing the bleachers, we turned to help build the sand volleyball court. Everyone had already been outside for eight hours; however, our task was not yet complete. We still had hundreds of pounds of sand to lug to the sand pit. Despite the humidity, we shoveled buckets and buckets of sand. We even began scooping it into garbage-can lids to take across the field and fill up the pit. A mixture of sweat, sand, and dirt covered our shirts. Around five o'clock, one of the supervisors told us that a contractor had agreed to fill the rest of the sand pit. "No, we want to finish," shouted the volunteers. We weren't just college-educated young people who could negotiate contracts with a construction company. We weren't just there to add to the existing center. The main reason we came was to inspire and empower the youth there by our willingness to pitch in and collaborate.

Throughout that experience, I learned a great deal about my fellow board members. We had all been accustomed to giving back to the community either individually at a local level, or together, through our funding meetings. But we had never performed direct service as a group. That day raised my estimation of the commitment and character of my companions. They combined the qualities that together I have suggested represent moral leadership: selflessness, genuineness, integrity, and empathy. They are some of the most humble people I have ever met, and are not afraid to venture out of comfortable meetings in the board room to share an important lesson about the power of collective action for the common good.

LESSON 6

Clear Goals Must Be Set in Civic Work

TOM AND ERNESTINE

Goals are essential in every job; if you don't know where you are going, it is never possible to know when you have arrived. In the private sector, the goals often differ from those in civic work. For a business, while customer and employee satisfaction are important, along with other goals such as protecting the environment, they are generally secondary. The need to make a profit is usually the primary focus. Put another way, few private companies can long survive without making a profit. Ernestine has had some experience in the for-profit sector, as she describes, and she has brought it to bear on the civic work that she has been doing. Tom, on the other hand, has worked only in government and nonprofit organizations. But together, we describe in this chapter the challenges of setting clear goals for civic work when there is no single focal point for measuring success.

As we discuss, the goals we have in mind are both organizational and personal. Tom grappled with the challenge of setting clear goals throughout his careers in public service—for instance, when he became the first head of the Legal Services Corporation. On the personal level, one of his times of civic self-reflection was when he had to choose whether the possible opportunity to be a federal appellate judge would best serve his commitment to public service. Ernestine has also faced the challenges of setting clear organizational goals, as, for example, when she initiated an entrepreneurship course at Stanford. She also had to decide which fork in the road to take along her personal civic path on numerous occasions starting with her founding of a nonprofit. Together our stories reflect the key role that setting clear goals has in effective civic work.

TOM

Government officials have a dominant duty to serve the public interest, but how to define that interest, how to know whether a particular action or inaction serves that interest, and how to measure success are all difficult questions, as we discuss in Lesson 2. Politicians running for office often have one set of answers as candidates and another set if they are elected. I have never run for elected office, but I have served officials who did: a governor, Foster Furcolo in Massachusetts, U.S. Presidents Kennedy, Johnson, and Carter in full-time positions, and George H. W. Bush and Clinton in part-time roles. These vantage points have given me perspective on the political pressures facing those in elected office to adopt policies seemingly far afield from their priorities in order to further those priorities. As I mention in Lesson 3, for example, I believe President Johnson escalated the war in Vietnam in significant part because he was concerned that otherwise he would not be able to gain Congressional approval of the "War on Poverty," which was Johnson's overriding concern.

Public-service positions do not have the counterpart to making a profit as a dominant goal. My experience underscores to me the essential requirement that civic leaders identify a small group of key objectives and then that those leaders stay focused on those objectives and not be distracted by challenges that are not on their primary agenda.

I began to learn this lesson as the new dean of Stanford Law School in 1971. I was 36 years old, and had been a law professor for the previous 6 years. That position offered little preparation for the deanship, but my predecessor, Bayless Manning, had tutored me for the last two years of his own deanship by appointing me to key positions in the School. One was to be chair of a committee to completely overhaul the curriculum. I learned on the job that the way to get this done was to include something significant in the revision that each group within the law faculty wanted. Over the course of 18 months, I listened hard to each faculty member and then was able to fashion a package of radical revisions that was adopted even though any one of them, taken alone, would have been voted down. This was invaluable preparation for the political dimensions of leadership.

When I became dean, Stanford Law School occupied the same building that it had been in since the founding of Stanford University in the 1890s. The building was a mess. My top priority, I knew, would be to raise the needed funds for a new set of buildings through the first capital campaign in the history of the School. In the process, I also hoped to gain support for endowed professorships, student scholarships, and the library. Stanford was seeking to join the ranks of leading law schools, but its financial support and its facilities were far behind those of its competitors. Its annual fund raised less than $100,000. When I started as dean, Manning gave me a list of about half the faculty and told me that all of those on the list were either being courted or could be courted by Harvard, Yale, and a few other top law schools. The prospect of losing up to half the faculty terrified me.

So the two key goals of my initial year as dean were clear and closely related to each other: succeeding in a major capital campaign, with a new set of buildings as the centerpiece of the campaign, and strengthening the ties of existing faculty to the School, while helping to attract strong new faculty. New facilities and a new set of endowed professorships would help to realize the second goal.

I set as a target for myself an ambitious fund-raising aim: to raise all the funds needed for four new, interconnected buildings—$12 million—by the end of my first year. (Little did I know, of course, that forty years later, my co-author, Ernestine, would be a student representative on the Trustees' Committee that approved new buildings on the campus.) These days, $12 million seems a modest amount. The Stanford Law School has already replaced one of the four buildings that resulted from the successful capital campaign in 1971, with a larger building at a total cost of about $85 million. But in 1971 Stanford Law School had never before had a major capital campaign. So the challenge was a substantial one.

Fortunately, I had some good tutors in successful fund raising who were part of the University's development office. I learned the essential lesson that people give to people and that I had to spend a great deal of time with each potential donor until that individual came to have confidence not only in Stanford Law School but in me as a person. Surprisingly to me, none of the major donors on the possible prospect list had attended the Law School, but each felt some tie to Stanford and to the field of law.

By late spring of 1972, we had raised $9 million for the new buildings. A recluse with ties to Stanford, though not the Law School, gave the key gift for a classroom building; the Kresge Foundation gave the funds for an auditorium; and smaller though substantial gifts covered the rest of the $9 million. The last and most important gift would be the final $3 million needed to complete the $12 million building fund. Colonel Henry Crown, patriarch of the Crown fortune in Chicago, was a likely prospect. His son, Robert, had gone to Stanford and had died as a young man. Another of his sons was a judge in Chicago and supported the notion of honoring his late brother by a gift to the School. I heard from him, however, that his father was insisting that for $3 million, the name of the School needed to be changed to the Crown Law School. I knew this was not a possibility.

I recall flying to Chicago cradling in my arms a large model of the four new buildings that would form the new facilities for the School. When I arrived at the office of Colonel Crown, I started to show him the model. He interrupted me with a question: "What will it cost?" I answered that the total cost would be $12 million for the four buildings that were planned and that we hoped that he and his family would give $3 million. "We'll do it," he responded, "but the name of the School needs to be changed to the Crown Law School." Having been prepared, I had my answer ready. "We can do better than that," I told him. "As you may know, the University of Michigan Law School is generally called 'Cooley Quadrangle,' and we will not only name the new library and office building 'the Robert Crown Building,' we will also name the whole complex of four new buildings 'Crown Quadrangle.'" Colonel Crown looked at me with the shadow of a smile and said, "Sold." And that was it.

Fortunately, along with raising the needed funds for the new Law School buildings, I was able to gain support for a number of new endowed professorships and for other critical needs of the School. This made the list of faculty who might jump to another school much less worrisome. But I did need to concentrate on hiring strong new faculty. As I indicate in Lesson 5, we hired the first woman faculty member at the School and the first Black faculty member. We also developed an affirmative action program to attract and retain strong minority student applicants. Other steps were included in my agenda as it evolved in the years that followed. But none of them would have been possible had my colleagues and I not succeeded in achieving our first two goals. This experience convinced me that in future public-service positions identifying a small number of primary goals at the outset, and then striving relentlessly to realize those goals, would be key to success.

The presidency of the Legal Services Corporation was my first position of leadership in government service. I knew that within a few weeks of taking office on January 1, 1976, I would need to fashion a budget proposal to Congress for the next fiscal year. As I write in Lesson 5, the federal program to support civil legal services had previously been part of the Office of Economic Opportunity in the White House, and for the five years of the Nixon administration, funding had been frozen while inflation had risen by over 30%. Increasing funding for legal services would be my key priority. I knew that an increase was essential if the new Corporation was to meet its statutory mandate to support legal services for people living below the poverty line.

My preliminary talks with members of Congress convinced me that we needed a simple message. About a third of the Congress would, I knew, be fully supportive of the program as long as we could show it was efficient and effective. Another third would never approve no matter how powerful our arguments. The middle third was key. Those members of Congress were skeptical, but my initial soundings persuaded me that we could gain their support if we could develop a simple message with a potent rationale. "More funding" alone would not satisfy those who were skeptical. The skeptics included both Democrats and Republicans.

Fortunately, Alf Corbett, the only person who came to the new Corporation from the old office of legal services in the White House helped find the answer. The Executive Vice President, Clint Bamberger, Corbett, and I struggled for most of a weekend when Corbett mentioned that there were eleven lawyers per 10,000 people in the United States, but far less than two lawyers per 10,000 poor people. I immediately realized that this potent fact could be the key to our fund-

ing request. We called it the "minimum access" plan. We wanted, over
the next four years, to increase funding for civil legal services in the
United States until there were at least two lawyers per 10,000 poor
people.

Fortunately, this seemingly simple solution worked marvelously. I
spent much of my first months as president of the Legal Services Corporation walking the halls of Congress talking one by one with Members and their staffs. "We are not asking for legal services at a level
equivalent to what is available to the rest of our citizenry," I stressed.
"We are only seeking 'minimum access'—less than a fifth of that
amount, or two lawyers per 10,000." This was the essence of the "minimum access plan," though we had to work out complex formulas so that
those sections of the country, particularly in the Northeast and on the
West coast, with more than this level would not be reduced. Indeed,
they too needed increases to cover inflation, though the increases could
not come as rapidly as new support for those sections of the country,
particularly in the South and Southwest, with little or no federal support.

We set this goal of "minimum access" as our target over a four-year
period. Congress supported the plan and within the four years funding
increased from $92.3 million to $321 million. At that point about 6,200
lawyers and 2,800 paralegals were serving in 323 programs throughout
the country. There were Congressional opponents, of course, but they
were largely confined to proposing restrictions on the abilities of legal-
services lawyers to provide help in specific areas of the law. From the
outset, these lawyers were precluded from work on matters involving
non-therapeutic abortions, selective service, and educational desegre-
gation. Each year we had to beat back efforts to expand that list, though
Congress did add a restraint on the representation of aliens known to be
in the U.S. illegally.

The overwhelming majority in Congress came in that brief period to
understand that our legal system could not operate fairly if poor people
were denied access because they were unable to afford the costs of a
private lawyer. We showed that most often these services were needed
because individuals living below the poverty line faced an acute crisis;
they were, for example, unlawfully fired from their jobs, removed as
tenants from their homes, or denied Social Security or unemployment
benefits. Our legal system depends, we successfully argued, on access.

Luckily, a significant share of moderate Republicans as well as Democrats were persuaded that funding legal services was a sound alternative to the blood on the streets—at least in a figurative sense—that could result from poor people being disenfranchised from the legal system. Most of those Republicans opposed other programs that resulted from President Johnson's War on Poverty. But they saw that legal services was different: it was "leveling the playing field" in an arena where access to justice was involved.

Even with "minimum access" secured, however, I knew that many poor people would be denied civil legal services unless members of the private bar agreed to give some of their time and talent pro bono to help those in need. A second key priority was to persuade private lawyers that this was an essential part of their responsibly. I argued that the public had granted them a monopoly on the delivery of legal services, and in return for that monopoly, the public was entitled to expect that poor people would be served without a fee. Bar associations throughout the country supported this view, as did the American Bar Association (ABA), and I worked closely with ABA leaders to strengthen legal services. Not every lawyer agreed, of course, and some accused me of demanding "involuntary servitude." But the general response from private lawyers was extremely positive.

When private lawyers were reluctant to give their time and talents to help poor people with legal problems, I found to my surprise that they often said, "I don't know anything about housing law, or Social Security benefits." And when I responded that we offered short courses that helped practicing lawyers learn what they needed to know in those fields, the lawyers said that "poor people would not be comfortable with me." What they really meant, I finally realized, was that they would not be comfortable talking with poor people because they had never done that, particularly if the poor people were Black or Brown. I came away from this experience convinced that educational opportunities were needed for students to engage with poor people, and this insight stayed with me when I returned to higher-educational administration.

A third key priority at the Legal Services Corporation was to work through these closely related issues: Why should taxpayers support civil legal services in relation to other public programs designed to help poor people? And since the funding available could not possibly cover all the legal needs of those people, how should the funds be allocated? I knew that the rationale for providing federal funding for civil legal services should be tied to the allocation process if it was to be persuasive as a matter of public policy. Strange as it may seem, virtually no attention was focused on the issue at the time the Legal Services Corporation was created. The hearings and debates in Congress on the Act that was finally adopted consumed several thousand pages. The structure of the Corporation, the ways in which the Board members would be chosen, and scores of procedural issues were endlessly debated. But the under-lying question—why legal services?—was not asked in any searching way.

In contrast to the closed room in which Corbett, Bamberger, and I devised the "minimum access" plan that served the Corporation so well, I thought it essential to have open and extended discussions about this "why" issue and its natural corollary, "How should limited funds be allocated?" by a legal-services program. If the answer to the "why" question is that legal services are an effective means to ameliorate pov-erty, then law reform should be a key, if not the primary, goal of those services. On the other hand, if the answer is that the hurdles imposed by the legal system should not be insurmountable due to poverty, then priority should be given to providing legal services in those situations when a client has no choice but to use those services—when one is sued, for example. We debated openly and at length these and other responses to the fundamental issue: Why should the federal govern-ment fund civil legal services for poor people?

Over the course of many months, the Board held extensive hearings on the issue. Councils made up of poor people were formed for each legal-services program and those Client Councils were asked to consid-er the matter. Ultimately, the Board and I concluded, with the full approval of those working in local programs, that priority should be determined by the Client Council for each program. As a result, hous-ing issues might be dominant in New York, for example, while indige-nous land claims were the priority in Hawaii. When we developed this approach, only one group vehemently opposed it: the Boston Bar Asso-ciation, which argued that clients could not possibly know enough to judge how scarce legal services should be allocated. But over time even that group came to accept our position.

These were not the only major issues that I dealt with as president of the Legal Services Corporation. It funded, for instance, a series of so-called "back-up centers" to help legal-services offices when faced with complex issues, particularly those dealing with reform of the legal system to help poor people. Conservatives in Congress were adamantly opposed to these centers, and their attack was led by a key member of Congress from Oregon, Edith Green. With the Board's acquiescence, we changed the names of these centers to "support centers" and announced that there would no longer be any "back-up centers." The ploy worked and the centers were able to continue their good work on behalf of the legal needs of indigents.

This and other tough matters involved time, energy, and effort for my three years as president of the Legal Services Corporation. Fortunately, this was a very successful time for the Corporation, one that legal-services lawyers often refer to as "the golden years." President Ford was in office for the first half of my tenure and President Carter for the second, but in both administrations the Corporation was able to gain substantially in funding and to maintain its independence from the White House. In the early months, in fact, the Ford administration tried to withdraw some of the funding that had been allocated, and we successfully sued the administration to keep that funding. This happened even before I was able to hire a full-time general counsel and my acting general counsel was a young lawyer in the firm of Hogan & Hartson, David Tatel, who later became a renowned judge on the U.S. Court of Appeals in Washington, D.C.

During my time in legal services, I was asked to consider whether I might want to stay in public service as a federal appellate judge. In 1978, the former dean of the Harvard Law School, Erwin Griswald, called to suggest allowing my name to be put forward for possible appointment to the U.S. Court of Appeals for the District of Columbia Circuit. Griswald was chair of a special committee appointed to screen nominees, and he said that my background was ideal for the job. I was flattered, but knew that my temperament was not suited to the role of a full-time judge. Even though I would be on the same judicial level as my mentor, Learned Hand, I realized that an appellate judge needs to be able to allow issues to be formulated for him and not to take a position except in response to opposing parties in a litigation. This would be too passive a role for me, I knew, much as I was attracted to a further career in public service.

I loved my public service as president of the Legal Services Corporation, where I learned in aching detail about the human face of poverty in America. I saw and heard first-hand the challenges poor people faced, challenges that too often were exacerbated rather than eased by the legal system. I visited legal-services programs in virtually every state in the country. This was an incredible learning experience for me.

I recall one time in Jackson, Mississippi, when two legal-services lawyers were in battle with the Governor and the entire Mississippi legal establishment about equal treatment for African Americans. I strategized with the legal-services lawyers one long night, and then met at breakfast the next day with leaders of the State Bar and former Mississippi Governor Ross Barnett, an ardent segregationist, to try to persuade them to change their strident opposition to integration. Barnett rebuffed my efforts, and insisted on telling me a series of racist stories.

Another time, I joined a couple of Alaskan legal-services lawyers in the Aleutian Islands. They had just won a lawsuit against the State of Alaska in the Alaska Supreme Court, and the Court's decision held that the State was required to provide high-school education to Eskimo children whose parents wanted them taught in their villages rather than in a high school on an Indian reservation in Oklahoma that was run by the Bureau of Indiana Affairs. I was fascinated as Inuit leaders argued back and forth in igloos about the pros and cons of these options.

These and scores of other experiences exposed me to the dedication and commitment of the lawyers and paralegals who worked to minimize the reality that justice was rationed in the United States. But I learned in the process that with so many worthy calls on limited resources, setting clear goals was essential to the successful operation of the Legal Services Corporation, just as it is in other realms of civic work.

ERNESTINE

It was an amusing sight, seeing a group of mostly thirty- and forty-year olds dressed in business suits or skirts and huddled around tables writing down their "life goals" for the next two years. I had read through the biographies of everyone in the room. One was a partner in a Canadian governmental health-care fund. Another was a three-time Olympian in swimming. A third was a university professor in entrepreneurship.

Glancing around the room, I felt out of place and inadequate—everyone was so accomplished.

I was half the age of many people in the room, but setting clear goals is important for people of all ages. We were all part of the Kauffman Fellows Program, which had been established under the Ewing Marion Kauffman Foundation and then shifted in 2003 to the auspices of the Center for Venture Education. It provides a two-year fellowship intended to foster investments in high-growth, high-impact entrepreneurial organizations around the world. About thirty of us had just been selected as the newest class of Kauffman Fellows, and this was our first meeting. Over the next few days, we spent a good deal of time getting to know one another, listening to talks from industry experts, taking personality tests, working on improvisation exercises, and—for a few hours—setting goals.

The goals of the Fellows varied widely. Some of those in the room were venture capitalists seeking high financial returns. Others sought to promote the social impact of their investments, such as by improving the environment. And still others focused on government funds that invested in private enterprises to further national agendas. We all had different individual objectives.

Next to me sat Julia Moore, associate director at the Stanford Institute for Innovation in Developing Economies, who wants to stimulate research and innovations to alleviate poverty in developing economies. Joanna Harris, the director of Endeavor Global, a nonprofit social entrepreneurial fund, is focused on growing Endeavor's footprint to include the Maghreb region in Northwest Africa and creating sustainable economic development through entrepreneurship. Both Julia and Joanna are devoted to fostering innovation in developing countries and using it as a solution to social issues.

Around the table where I sat were also a number of people involved in government, each with different goals. John Lisko is the Chief Investment Officer for the Pennsylvania State Treasurer, and he wants to ensure responsible management of $12 billion in U.S. Treasury investment pools. Anh Nguyen is a medical officer at the U.S. Food and Drug Administration National Institutes of Health, and he has a particular interest in identifying why some prospective medical products fail before they reach the market, the solution to which could save companies millions of dollars.

The group also included more traditional venture capital investors such as Dan Janiak who had been an associate at In-Q-Tel, a nonprofit firm, as I mention in Lesson 1, that invests in information technology, and then decided to work at the Texas branch of Draper Fisher Jurvetson, a venture-capital firm. As I struggled to articulate my own goals that day, I recalled my initial meeting with the State Farm® Youth Advisory Board, a meeting that helped me decide to focus much of my future civic efforts on supporting youth.

The State Farm® Youth Advisory Board was my first experience being involved with a corporate culture. As I mentioned previously, I had been asked to serve on this Board, which makes decisions about allocating $5 million annually for youth service projects. State Farm® would pay all my hotel and travel expenses to come to these board meetings. My initial reaction was that the role of the Board was created just to give the Company cover while it made the decisions. I expected a group of adults to be running the show, while a group of youth would be following their lead. I assumed that this was just a way for State Farm® to fulfill its corporate social responsibility, while appearing to be forward-thinking. I could not imagine that young people would be given the power to make State Farm® funding decisions.

I remember heading by taxi in the middle of the night from the airport in Chicago to a hotel booked at the last minute. It was so cold outside that the cab driver did not even bother to get out and help me with my luggage. Earlier that day, my flight had been delayed, and I had to spend many hours sitting in the airport.

To my surprise and pleasure, the meeting that started early the next morning was key to helping me formulate my own core goal of helping young people achieve their potential. My excitement in coming to this realization made the hurdles of getting to the meeting seem trivial. It was only when the meeting got underway that the aims of the State Farm® Youth Advisory Board became clear, and with that clarity came an epiphany about myself and my own personal goal. I recall taking an elevator to the fourteenth floor and then walking up a winding staircase, to a board room that overlooked downtown Bloomington, Illinois, and the rounded top of the city hall with tall Roman columns.

It suddenly hit me that I was with peers from across the country, a group of youth sitting around a table that was periodically occupied by the CEO of State Farm® and his board of directors. For the first time I understood that State Farm® had provided the Board members with real decision-making power. We had the ability to empower other youth. It was up to me and the other young people on the Board to use that power wisely.

All the civic projects that my fellow Board members and I considered were proposed and led by young people. The experience of reviewing these projects during my years on the Board gave me a wide-angle lens to see an incredible range of ways that young people were working to enhance the lives of others. Since I left the Board, a number of powerful young leaders have succeeded me, many of whom I highlight throughout this book. They also focus on youth-led service projects. Helping and fostering youth—whether as a peer, investor, volunteer, or friend—has since been central to my identity. It is reflected in my nonprofit work, in my student government and civic activities at Stanford, and in my venture capital role when I seek out possible investments in projects proposed by young people.

Of course, setting clear goals in civic work, as in other realms, is easier said than done. Hardships along the way are more the rule than the exception. But as I have seen in my own civic work and that of my peers, difficulties can be mitigated or overcome, as long as you keep your key goals center-stage in your mind.

Alok Vaid-Menon, an Indian gay rights activist and an undergraduate at Stanford, had received death threats because of his activism. When Alok became co-president of Stanford Students for Queer Liberation, he set the goal of changing how homophobic students viewed queer people and queer rights. He had heard about the suicides of gay students caused by their sense of a dominant culture of homophobia amongst his peers. Alok wanted to spark conversations about both sexuality and race at Stanford, and what should be considered as "norms" among Stanford students. He began plastering his dorm hallways and doorways with signs such as, "White Privilege: I know that there will always be history classes that address my history" and "Heterosexual Privilege: I don't have to come out as straight." He felt that posting such provocative signs about homosexuality and racial prejudice would challenge assumptions that white and heterosexual identities and experiences were superior.

Alok and his signs certainly sparked conversation – but not exactly the ones he had hoped for. Hours after posting these signs, Alok's full name was released online by the *Stanford Review*. Those who disliked these signs were quickly able to find Alok's contact information, from searching the Internet, and Alok began to receive threatening messages:

> "Nature will reject that which has no worth, from a homosexual deviant to a junkies babies birth. Just keep that in mind, Queer Liberation Group."
> "I can't stand queers who want us to openly accept and tolerate their pervasive and sickening lifestyles in the most heinous of fashions. This queer liberation group is nothing more than an immoral parasite destroying the remaining moral fabric of this once great nation. Someone should 'liberate' them for good, if you know what I mean."
> "Oh believe me—we know we're not the norm! You can rest assured of that, Alok Vaid-Menon."

It is hardly surprising that Alok was shocked. Initially, the threats were only a trickle, and Alok was unsure how seriously he should take them. "At first I was afraid to return to campus," Alok said to me. When Alok did return, he met with both the leaders of the Stanford advising office and the Stanford police for safety precautions, "I felt I was directly being threatened," he told me.

Fortunately, not every civic work experience has the same dark side as that of Alok, but the lesson he learned is applicable to all public service: There will be barriers and hurdles you must overcome in order to achieve your goals. Rather than let threats deter him, Alok decided to remember the big picture: he started dialogues and conversations all over the campus. It also helped that many queer activists praised him for his work, telling him that he had helped them.

As Alok realized, when striving towards your goals, focus on the positive, rather than the negative aspects. Things will not always go smoothly. In the words of Sumat Lam, another student with whom Tom and I spoke, "Don't give up because it's all about how persistent you are and how much you believe you can make a difference." If you persist, then at the end of the day, you will realize that you made a change, you made a difference.

Sometimes, it is difficult even to start creating change in your civic work, especially when administrative regulations and bureaucracy stand in the way, as I realized when visiting for the first time Gateways Hospital and Mental Health Center in Los Angeles as part of my music-making for VAMS on New Year's Day.

We were stripped of our usual holiday decorations, our sparkly black heels, velvet trimmed reindeer ears, pure white plastic snowmen, multi-colored kazoos, and other cheer-makers. Within thirty minutes of entering Gateways Hospital and Mental Health Center, I was pulled aside for "potentially endangering the patients." Our strident noisemakers, sharp-edged music stands, and even the lengthy ribbons that adorned our gifts, were considered risky.

I stood in the circle of volunteers, nervously shifting back and forth. I felt bare. All the colorful holiday mishmash we had devoted hours to preparing was going to waste. "Do you all remember why we're here?" I asked, unsure if I knew the answer myself. After a few attempts at gallows humor—"because we want to party" and "because Ernestine forced us here,"—there was a serious silence. "To make the people here happy!" one student said. "Exactly," I smiled, although at the time, I was just trying to put on a brave show. "We don't need decorations to do that."

In some ways, I felt like a convict that day. It was the first day of a new year and not many volunteers joined me. The ones who did join were eyed closely. Eight of us carefully trailed a security guard as he unlocked a metal-barred door and stood at the side, cautiously watching us as we walked through. His counterpart unlocked the second door, an entrance that was a bit more welcoming, but nonetheless also guarded by a wary man in a uniform.

In the eyes of the guards, my friends and I were not responsible adults. We might be dangerous. Every step seemed tougher than I expected when I started VAMS as a nonprofit organization designed to bring music to people particularly in need of some joy in their lives. Bureaucratic hurdles appeared to delay all that we tried to do. Everything required approval from several tiers of administrators—sticklers who seemed more concerned with following needless rules than with the welfare of their patients and clients. Administrative issues often piled up, one after another, until the time of our volunteer events, and sometimes even during them.

Now looking at the boxes brimming with unused decorations that sit in a large pile in the corner of my garage, I remember when Leah Worthington, a student-government leader at Palo Alto High School with whom Tom and I spoke, told me, "One big thing I had to learn was to simplify, to go back to basics." I had gained this insight myself when visiting Gateways Hospital and Mental Health Center. The time with patients there was not all about the flashy decorations, but rather simply about putting a smile on the faces of a group of mentally-ill adolescents and adults.

Kimberly Conner, another Stanford student with whom Tom and I talked, encountered similar problems when performing public service. She realized that carefully organized goals and arrangements may be out of your individual control—left in tatters—and backup plans can fall apart. She told us about working one summer in Bolivia with an indigenous youth group in Tiraque, a small town at the top of a mountainous region and difficult to reach.

One of the community's most pressing problems was garbage disposal. The village had trash in the store corners, streets, and seemingly everywhere. Villagers had no way to collect garbage and transport it back down the mountain. Realizing that the health of the community was at risk if the trash remained there, Kimberly decided to organize a community beautification event. She wanted to create an environmental campaign that would give incentives to youth in Tiraque to organize trash cleanups. Youth who collected the most amount of trash were to be awarded prizes.

Donned in latex gloves and armed with black trash bags, dozens of youth paced the streets of Tiraque, hunching over every few minutes to collect cardboard boxes, tattered napkins, and stained cups. After a long day of hard work, Kimberly and her volunteer group had a large pile of black garbage bags filled to the brim and piled up in a corner of the town. As the young volunteers sat down to rest and call it a successful day, one of the project leaders exclaimed in a worried voice, "There's nowhere to put these bags, and we don't have the means to transport them down the mountain," pointing to the large pile of bags as he spoke. He was right. Having the garbage collected in bags was a lot better for the health of the people of Tiraque, but without a means to take the bags down the mountain, Kimberly had not solved this pressing civic problem.

Sometimes, solutions to civic concerns are simply out of your control. When Kimberly first engaged in public service, one of the hardest ideas for her to accept was that no matter how fervently she pursued a project or how passionately she devoted herself to a cause, her impact was often dictated by outside factors that were beyond her power. She wanted the youth in Tiraque to realize this, to accept this reality. So she told them the following parable of a great forest fire:

> The terrible fire raged and burned. All of the animals were afraid and fled from their homes. The elephant and the tiger, the beaver and the bear all ran, and above them the birds flew in a panic. Only Dukdukdiya, the little hummingbird, would not abandon the forest. Dukdukdiya flew quickly to the stream. She picked up a single drop of water in her beak. Dukdukdiya flew back and dropped the water on the fire. Again she flew to the stream and brought back another drop, and so she continued—back and forth, back and forth. The other animals watched Dukdukdiya's tiny body fly against the enormous fire, and they were frightened. They called out to the little hummingbird, warning her of the dangers of the smoke and the heat. "What can I do?" sobbed the rabbit. "This fire is much too hot." "There is too much smoke!" howled the wolf. "My wings will burn! My beak is too small!" cried the owl. But the little hummingbird persisted. She flew to and fro, picking up more water and dropping it, bead by bead, onto the burning forest. Finally the big bear said, "Little Dukdukdiya, what are you doing?" Without stopping, Dukdukdiya looked down at all of the animals. She said, "I am doing what I can."

The parable reminded her, Kimberly said, that while we may be limited in our own contributions, if we all are courageous enough to do what we can, together we will wield a great power to better the world. Kimberly had engaged the youth of an entire community, but at the end of the day, there was still a huge garbage problem. Often, you may not have met all your original intentions, but you may well have inspired someone else to do more than would have otherwise happened.

Luckily, rather than lose hope, the Tiraque youth and other villagers came together as a group and refocused their energies to find a solution with Kimberly. They decided to redefine what success for that day was: building trust among themselves and developing important relationships within the community. They discussed what they could do as a result of having met this goal, and soon enough they were able to resolve the garbage-bag disposal problem through personal connections. They were able to talk with city officials and find large dump-trucks to remove all the garbage bags.

Kimberly's success reminds me of the time when I reconnected with Bruce Neckels two years after graduating high school. We were having a quick breakfast at Dupar's Restaurant in Studio City, the same place where I first met him approximately four years earlier when he decided to introduce me to Mike Klausman, whom I mention in Lesson 1. As I sat in a red leather chair, pretending to glance over the brunch menu although I already knew exactly what I wanted, one question circulated in my head, "Why did he decide to support me?" I was only fifteen years old when I first met Bruce, and I had some crazy ideas and big needs.

"Do you know the story of Emma Kunkle Divine?" Bruce began.

Emma was seventeen years old when she began volunteering for the Salvation Army in 1901. Emma was sent to the New York Bowery district to attract street donations, but no one wanted to donate when she at first passively sat in front of a large black donation kettle. Rather than give up, Emma walked across the street to a five and dime store, bought a bell with a handle for a nickel, and started loudly ringing it the next day. As she did, several people began dropping money into the kettle.

"When I first met you," Bruce said, "It's like you were ringing a bell, and I had to answer it. You were ringing it so loud and clear that I immediately realized that you had a passion for aiding others. There was no way I could not help you." No matter how young we are or who we are, we all have a bell to ring, and if we ring it loudly enough and if it is for a noble cause, people will hear. Make your goals loud and clear.

LESSON 7

Civic Work Should Be Its Own Reward

TOM AND ERNESTINE

All of us like to be thanked when we do something that helps others. In this Lesson, we explain why those of us who do civic work should not expect gratitude from those in need of help, though we may enjoy it when it comes our way. Particularly when our civic work helps those in difficult circumstances, financial or otherwise, it is often difficult for them to express more than their sorrow at those circumstances, which may be mixed with envy for those in a position to help them.

Each of us has been thanked, of course, by people whom we have helped though our civic work, and we do not suggest that we were other than deeply moved on occasions when that has occurred. Ernestine tells one such tale at the close of Lesson 2 when she quotes the beautiful message she received from an elderly woman when she and her friends ran a Valentine's Day Bingo Tournament at a senior center. In Lesson 5, Tom tells of the compliment he was given by Secretary of State Dean Rusk when he handled a difficult assignment.

At the same time, both of us have found that the satisfaction of helping others, of reaching out to those in need, and of being part of something larger than ourselves, are the real rewards of civic work, not expressions of gratitude, let alone awards for civic work. We do that work because it is part of who we are, and we feel fortunate to have the privilege of public service.

TOM

Over the course of my professional careers, I frequently met men and women who had been successful in the private sector and who told me that they wanted to "give back" by engaging in civic work. They often sought positions in the federal government, and the more successful they had been in their prior work the higher the governmental appointment that they expected to hold. Many of those people failed in their efforts, for thousands of individuals have the hope of a high-level federal position, particularly a presidential appointment, and there are only a limited number of these. There are far fewer jobs that report directly to the president.

Among those who do succeed in obtaining a senior position in the federal government, I often found that they expected to be applauded and thanked for their civic work, particularly by those who benefited directly from that work. My experience in legal services taught me, however, that civic work should be viewed as its own reward and the chances of being honored or even thanked for that work are often minimal. One should not expect gratitude from those being served, but rather experience intrinsic pleasure from the work for its own sake. This lesson came home to me powerfully in my last full-time government post.

I would have stayed longer as president of the Legal Services Corporation, but I was also ambitious to have a job that reported directly to the president and thought I might never have another opportunity if I did not try to gain that position then, while President Carter was in office. Many of my friends had been eager for such an appointment and had failed in their quest.

Fortunately for me, Warren Christopher was Deputy Secretary of State at the time, the same position that George W. Ball had held, though the title changed from Under Secretary, and I knew Christopher well since he was a Stanford Law School graduate and strong supporter of the School. He had also been extremely helpful to me from his position as head of the Los Angeles Bar Association when I was at the Legal Services Corporation. Cyrus Vance was the Secretary of State then, and he, too, was a good friend, for he had been head of the Bar of the City of New York and also supportive of legal services for the poor.

One day in 1978, Christopher called me and said that President Carter would like to appoint me as the first head of a new agency, reporting directly to the President and with policy responsibility for all aspects of foreign assistance, both unilateral and bilateral. The Agency for International Development (AID) would be under my jurisdiction along with U.S. policy for the World Bank and the regional development banks. I would be in charge of shaping U.S. development policies relating to all third-world countries. This was the chance that I had been hoping for, and I did not hesitate to accept. A primary opportunity would be to work directly for President Carter, whom I admired. I also knew a good deal about third-world development and foreign aid for I had taught international economic development with a Stanford Business School professor as a joint course for law and business students, and I found the field fascinating.

I only later learned that the reorganization that would create the new agency, the International Development Cooperation Agency (IDCA), had not yet been approved by Congress and that there was significant opposition among both Republicans and Democrats. The opponents argued that the reorganization would simply create a new layer of federal bureaucracy on top of already large and lumbering bureaucracies. When Christopher asked me to accept the position he told me that my job would be to coordinate policy, not to be responsible for operating programs, and that an Assistant Secretary of State, Doug Bennett, would leave that position and take charge of the Agency for International Development. Naturally, we would both be subject to Senate confirmation, and I would have four positions under me that would be appointed by the President and subject to Senate confirmation.

Luckily, Senator Jacob Javits of New York, a prominent liberal Republican, was a co-sponsor of the reorganization bill along with many Democrats. Lee Hamilton, Democratic Congressman from Indiana, was head of the House Foreign Relations Committee, and a strong backer of the reorganization. We became friends as we worked together on foreign-aid issues, and our friendship deepened when I went to his home state as president of Indiana University. Congress ultimately approved the reorganization, though not without a tough struggle. President Carter was never a popular president with the Congress, and his proposals, such as this one, suffered as a result. Subsequently, Bennett and I were both approved by the Senate and we began work together.

The President proposed the Agency, as he told me, because he found there was little coordination between the Agency for International Development, which is the major U.S. bilateral foreign-aid agency; other bilateral-aid programs such as Food for Peace, which is run by the Department of Agriculture; and the multilateral-aid efforts, including the World Bank and the regional banks, such as the Inter-American Development Bank. Further, President Carter said, U.S. development policies ought to be coordinated with U.S. international trade policies and with other U.S. international policies. The President told me that these were my responsibilities and that he would back me.

President Carter made clear to me that his priorities were long-term economic development on the one hand and human rights on the other. These were to be my priorities in decision-making on foreign aid and fortunately, they were priorities that I thought were exactly the right ones. For too long, I believed, the United States had supported regimes through foreign aid that abused human rights and gave foreign aid to further short-term foreign policy interests rather than to promote long-term development prospects. This would be a wonderful chance to put my beliefs into practice.

What I did not fully appreciate until I had been on the job for a few months was that while Bennett, as the head of the Agency for International Development, was in charge of a budget of several billion dollars, I was in charge of one that involved only a few dozen staff members. I could choose four people to work with me who would all have presidential appointments, which meant they also would have to be approved by the Senate, but I had no budget muscle to back up my judgments. I also realized only later that each presidential appointee is subject to what is termed a "full-field investigation" by the F.B.I., a process that takes many months. As a result, some of those I wanted to choose for these positions would not leave their private firms for an appointment that might be less than two years.

I still have in my office a signed picture of President Carter shaking hands with me. Underneath is a letter he sent to me with these words:

"Tom: You are the boss. Act boldly re bureaucratic coordination and efficiency. I'll back you up. Keep me informed re problems & progress." In fact, however, as I slowly began to realize, few in the upper levels of federal officialdom other than President Carter really supported the two priorities that he had given me. As a practical matter, my job was to step into other agencies' responsibilities and to tell them that they could not do what they wanted to do because their proposed actions or inactions were inconsistent with President Carter's priorities.

My friends Warren Christopher and Cyrus Vance, Secretary and Deputy Secretary of State, were deeply committed to international human rights and were architects of a powerful set of policies in that arena that shaped U.S. policies in important ways and made the U.S. a moral exemplar to the rest of the world. But they both also had responsibility for handling scores of hot spots around the world, and foreign-aid money was one of the ways to do that handling. U.S. ambassadors in Third World countries might understand the President's priorities, but they had to deal with the governments in the countries where they were stationed, and foreign-aid money was often the "coin of the realm."

I recall a visit to Brazil, for example, where I stayed at the residence of the U.S. Ambassador at the start of an extended trip throughout South America. The ambassador wanted to use U.S. foreign aid as a carrot to persuade the Brazilian Government to support one of our foreign-policy objectives—I forget which one—while I insisted that the aid was available only for promoting long-term economic development in Brazil. By the end of my visit, the ambassador was furious with me. When I left, he called together all his senior staff and presented me with a heavy onyx ashtray as a parting gift, knowing full well that I did not smoke, that I was not checking any of my luggage on airlines when I travelled, and that the ten-pound ashtray was the last thing I needed, but that I would be forced to carry it throughout South America and back to the U.S. Only sometime later was I able to realize the humor of his move.

Difficult as my hurdles were in terms of U.S. bilateral aid, those involving multilateral aid were even more challenging. The Treasury Department had long been the decision-maker in dealing with the World Bank and the regional banks. The Secretary of the Treasury and his colleagues had no interest in allowing a young upstart to horn in on their prerogatives. The same was true of the Department of Agriculture in terms of food aid, and for the U.S. Special Trade Representative, who was responsible for U.S. trade policy. I found that with one exception—an assistant to the President named Henry Owen—the President's staff was not deeply committed to furthering the two priorities he had set for IDCA and for me. Their primary concern in the last two years of President Carter's first term in office was ensuring that there would be a second term, and foreign-aid policy did not even register on the political priority list.

To my surprise, President Carter called me directly a number of times to express his interest in a particular foreign-aid project or to ask me what could be done to promote the development of a country in which he was interested. Mali, I recall, was one of those countries. It had the lowest per-capita income of any country in Africa and was of absolutely no strategic interest to the United States. But President Carter knew of the pressing poverty facing the country and wanted to help. Moreover he read carefully each of my budget proposals and even sat in on some of my budget presentations to the staff of the Office of Management and Budget. In retrospect, as I mentioned, President Carter has been criticized for being a micro-manager, too closely involved in the details of management and not enough of a strategic thinker. And this is a fair criticism. On the other hand, he represented American idealism and values in a way that we had not previously seen in the years after the Kennedy administration and did not see again during the Reagan years.

The result of my bureaucratic position, and the waning influence of President Carter with Congress, meant that this civic work, unlike my other government positions, was not enjoyable. In fact, my leadership of IDCA is the only position I have held in any organization that was not fun. The bureaucratic infighting, particularly with the Treasury Department, was too intense and difficult. I found that I could challenge other agency heads with my mandate from the President, but that this move would often not succeed. I could not simply send an angry note to the President and expect a prompt response. Rather, I had to prepare a memorandum explaining why the step I wanted taken, or prevented, was furthering the President's priorities. Someone in the White House would then ask the agency head who took a different position to write a memorandum explaining that position. Then the White House staff person would write what was called "an options paper" that spelled out each of our positions, and frequently there were a number of agencies involved so there would be multiple positions. The President was asked to endorse one of the options. Needless to say, the way the options paper was written had everything to do with how the President decided the matter. My one strong ally on the White House staff, Henry Owen, was no match for the combined bureaucratic muscle of the other agency heads, and I lost more often than I won. Too often, I, along with others involved, saw the whole process in terms of winning and losing, rather than furthering the public interests of the United States.

The IDCA experience did give me a chance to travel to Third World countries in Africa, Asia, and Latin America. I headed delegations of U.S. officials from many agencies to international conferences and helped set policies at those conferences. I stayed at the U.S. ambassadorial residences in scores of countries. I learned a great deal about poverty throughout the world to supplement my knowledge through legal services of poverty in the U.S. And I came to have a deep appreciation for the wisdom, dedication, and hard work of women and men who made the U.S. foreign service or the civil service the civic work of their lives.

But the job was not fun, and I came to appreciate, more fully than I had before, how important it is to have fun in one's work; not every day, of course; no one could reasonably ask for that. But one should find pleasure most of the time. I felt satisfaction because I believed deeply in the goals of the President, but much of my time I found was just engaged in hard, bureaucratic slogging.

Perhaps most important, I came to see—as I had in heading the Legal Services Corporation—that one should not expect gratitude from civic work, but rather view it as its own reward. The United States allocated billions of dollars in foreign assistance while I was head of the International Development Cooperation Agency, and I had a chance to help shape the impact of that aid on poverty-stricken people in Third-World countries. Those people no doubt appreciated the help they were receiving, but they rarely expressed their gratitude. Rather, as I heard one elderly woman tell me in Indonesia, she and her family resented the grinding poverty that was their lot, and saw with some anger how much better off were most of those in the United States. Why did the accident of their birth, she said in effect to me, doom them to lives that were "nasty, brutish, and short," as Thomas Hobbes put it several centuries ago. So she took our food help, and she realized full-well that she was better off with that help than she would have been without it, but those of us in the United States could not and should not expect her gratitude.

There were offsetting moments during my time as head of the International Development Cooperation Agency that helped keep me amused some of the time, including several that involved getting used to the ways of the rural Georgians who were in the President's inner circle of advisors. I recall sitting with a small group of White House staff members including two of the President's principle assistants, Jodie Powell and Hamilton Jordan. They were drinking Coca Cola and, after pouring their drinks from cans, would open bags of peanuts, shake the contents of the bags into their glasses, and then eat the peanuts at the same time they drank—a sight to behold, I thought! On another occasion, I was seated at breakfast in an elegant White House dining room next to President Carter and watched while he took a large helping of grits with melted butter on top. I wrestled with whether my influence would wane even further if I declined the grits—which I did.

The high point of the social side of my position was a state dinner in the White House for the president of Nigeria. I was not seated with anyone particularly interesting, but my wife Ellen sat next to former Governor Averell Harriman, a hero to both of us. We admired him for many reasons. One was that after a long and distinguished career he agreed to join the State Department as Assistant Secretary of State because he thought he could still contribute in the service of his country. At the end of the dinner my wife asked Governor Harriman for his place card as a keepsake. "Only, Mrs. Ehrlich," he said without a moment's hesitation, "if I may have yours." These were among the moments that added luster to the job.

On the other hand, I did come to strengthen my views about the importance of each lesson that Ernestine and I discuss in this book, not just that civic work should be its own reward. For example, I realized even more clearly than before that leadership in civic work requires a firm focus on key goals. I began many meetings I had with other agency officials, and also ones with foreign government representatives, by stressing the twin mandates that President Carter had given me. I insisted that whatever particular policy was being proposed had to further one or both of those objectives or it would not involve U.S. bilateral or multilateral aid. This did not make me popular. I can still remember then Assistant Secretary of State Richard Holbrooke, a man for whom I gained enormous respect, exploding in anger because I was blocking what I viewed as his demand for "walking around money" for some African leader. In Holbrooke's view, of course, the funds were essential to persuade that leader to do something Holbrooke thought was in U.S. interests.

In November 1980, Ronald Reagan ended President Carter's bid for a second term, and I had to think of my own next career steps. My colleagues and I, in a spirit of bipartisanship, prepared detailed briefing materials for the new administration explaining the main goals of the International Development Cooperation Agency, and the ways that those goals could be realized in the years ahead. But the "transition team" assigned by President-elect Reagan had no interest in long-term development assistance or in human rights. In effect, the new agency was scrapped in all but name, and foreign aid was focused solely on furthering national security vis-à-vis the Soviet Union.

I had assumed that I would go back to Stanford as a law professor, though I had ambitions to help lead a university. Several opportunities had come along in prior years, but those that I was extremely interested in did not work out and I rejected others for which I might have been chosen. In all events, it made no sense to leave Washington in January 1981, since two of our younger children were still in school there. So I arranged to be a visiting scholar at the Brookings Institution in Washington, taking a sabbatical from Stanford University, something that I had never been able to do in my eleven years there.

During my time at Brookings I was able to write about the two civic work arenas in which I had engaged over the past five years: legal services and foreign aid. To my sorrow, the Reagan administration quickly set about trying to eliminate federal support for legal services as well as to focus foreign aid solely in support of U.S. military security. At Brookings I was able to write both policy articles and op-ed pieces, and to reflect on the civic work experiences that I had and how I might further civic work when I returned to higher education. As I reflected, the lessons in this book began to take shape in my mind.

In the spring of 1981, I was considered to be provost at the University of Pennsylvania, my mother's alma mater. Ellen and I spent an evening with Sheldon Hackney, the new president of the University, and his wife Lucy, and we came away convinced that this was a great opportunity. Penn, for most of its two-hundred year history since its founding by Benjamin Franklin, had a provost but no president, and the position of provost was perhaps the strongest of any among leading universities. It included responsibility for all academic affairs such as promotion and tenure decisions, and all student affairs, along with budgetary authority in those areas. I quickly accepted Hackney's offer to join him. Almost as soon as I arrived at Penn as provost, I began to think about the ways that higher education could promote interest among students in civic work.

As I wrote earlier, several years after I came to Philadelphia, my daughter went to work for a brand new national organization of college and university presidents, Campus Compact. It was given its name by one of my public-service mentors, John W. Gardner. Campus Compact was created because a small group of leaders in higher education thought that "the me generation"—one of the labels of the 1980s for college students—was unfair to them. These leaders believed that their students should have opportunities for civic work and committed themselves to providing those opportunities. Because my daughter was involved, I quickly became interested and engaged in Campus Compact and its efforts. I recalled my sense that students needed direct experiences working to help those in need, and I saw Campus Compact as a means to promote these experiences.

Meanwhile, as provost at Penn I gained a good sense of how to lead academic planning at a large research university. The job was a wonderful one for me and I loved my work there. Sheldon and Lucy Hackney became two special friends for Ellen and me. My collaboration with Sheldon was a particular source of pleasure. And I found I could become close friends with several of Penn's deans even though they reported to me.

After six years at Penn, I thought I was ready to be a university president and I wanted that opportunity. I was especially eager to lead a public university, to return to public service. Indiana University offered a particularly exciting opportunity, I thought, because its Board of Trustees wanted a new president who would focus on enhancing the academic strengths of the University. My experience at Penn had prepared me to take on just that responsibility. At the same time, it offered all the challenges of a Big Ten institution: about 100,000 students on eight campuses and a budget of about $2.5 billion. My focus would need to be not only on academic excellence, but also on access to college for all those who wanted to attend and on promoting Indiana's economic development. The campuses at Bloomington and Indianapolis were major research centers, and the other six campuses were opportunity centers for commuting students to gain the higher education they needed. All eight campuses were economic engines for their regions and the State.

I felt fortunate to be chosen as president of Indiana University in the spring of 1987. This was a courageous move on the part of the University Board and search committee for I was a liberal from the East Coast, a Jew, wore bow ties, and had never been involved with a public university. The State was dominantly conservative, and of the five and a half million residents, only 25,000 were Jews. And virtually no men there wore bow ties! But the University Trustees felt that the University had been drifting downhill in academic terms, and they chose me because they thought I could reverse that trend.

It also took a bit of courage, I think, for Ellen and me to make the move. But we felt so warmly welcomed that we not only had no regrets, we frequently told each other how fortunate we were to be in Indiana and living on the stunningly beautiful Bloomington campus. From the start, we were able to do much of the work together, a pleasure we had not had before. The presidency of any university is a visible position, but the presidency of a major public university is particularly visible. Ellen and I delighted in being able to collaborate in dealing with the State legislature, in fund-raising, and in working with the multiple constituencies of Indiana University. Our move brought us together as working partners in new and wonderful ways.

It was hard to walk down any street in the State without seeing someone who graduated from the University or whose son or daughter was a student there. Everyone in the State viewed it with pride as "their University," and it was my responsibility to ensure that they could strengthen that pride through strengthening the academic enterprise. Before I took the job, I met with the Republican Governor, Robert Orr. I wanted to be sure that my own background in Democratic administrations in Washington would not hurt the University. He assured me that he viewed the University as a nonpartisan asset for the State, which was exactly my position.

As president of Indiana University, I was able to put into practice the lessons outlined in this book that I had learned in my prior administrative positions. Ellen and I were treated with warmth almost everywhere we went, and I often felt a palpable sense of pride in Indiana University among the thousands of Hoosiers we met. But we both also relearned the key lesson that civic work should be its own reward. We were often thanked for what the University was doing. But we also clearly saw, as had been true in my prior public-service roles, that it is never wise to expect gratitude, let alone depend on it, to make civic work deeply satisfying and fulfilling.

Even before I took office, I began a complex academic planning effort for all eight campuses focused on undergraduate education, graduate education, research, and statewide economic development. These would be my priorities for all the years when I was president. I worked to tie each of these four key areas to academic objectives on the one hand and direct benefits to the State on the other. I also learned how to work closely with the State legislature and the Indiana Higher Education Commission, which was responsible for coordination of academic programs.

At Indiana University, I relearned a lesson that has been with me since my first position in civic work: any leader will inevitably fail to realize some of his or her objectives, as Ernestine discusses in Lesson 6. The signature of a wise leader is to learn from the failure, something that is often easy to forget when one is still smarting from the wounds of a losing battle.

A minor example occurred in the fall of my first year as president of Indiana University. The Bloomington athletic department wanted a new scoreboard for the football stadium, and it presented me with a proposal that the costs of a fancy scoreboard would be entirely paid for by a major Indiana company. In exchange, the company's name and logo would be prominently displayed on the scoreboard. I was worried about the commercialization of many aspects of higher education, including athletics, but reluctantly agreed as long as the company also paid for a large electronic sign on the main road into the campus. That sign (which would have no mention of the company) could carry messages about events on the campus and other information of interest to visitors.

At one of my first Faculty Council meetings, several faculty members stood up and objected to this proposed highway sign, saying that they thought it marred the beauty of the campus. I defended my decision to have the sign, but objections grew both louder and more numerous, not only from faculty but also from others in the community. After several weeks, I reversed course and issued a public statement saying that I made a mistake in wanting the sign and that it would not be displayed as planned.

I also said that I would try to learn from my mistake and engage in more consultation in the future before taking another such step again. The fact that I said publicly that I made a mistake and would work to correct it gained me immeasurable credit. Ironically, making a mistake proved to help me in promoting my main agenda of strengthening the academic standards in the University.

As in prior positions, I focused on key goals. I soon concluded that the Trustees were right: the University had been drifting academically, and all my goals were academic ones. The faculty was generally very supportive, as was the Board. That governing body was a small one, only nine members, including one student, and over time I learned that if more than one became a problem to me, I would have difficulty leading. But I was fortunate in that the chair of the Board was a wonderful man, Dick Stoner, executive vice president at Cummins Engine, one of the largest companies in the State, and an active Democrat who was reappointed to the Board by Republican governors as well as Democratic ones. The vice-chair of the Board was an active Republican lawyer from Indianapolis, Harry Gonzo, a hero in the State because he had been quarterback of the only Indiana football team in recent years to play in the Rose Bowl. Stoner and Gonzo were a wonderful, collaborative team, and they supported my efforts for the first several years of my term as president.

Just after my appointment was announced, I received a copy of the University calendar for the upcoming year and I realized that Homecoming was scheduled on Yom Kippur. I immediately called Stoner and told him that I could not participate in Homecoming unless the date was altered. He did not hesitate to make the change. Jewish faculty and staff learned of this and many contacted me to express their gratitude.

Sometimes, I found, politics clashed with academic priorities. One step that the Medical School dean and I wanted to take, for example, was to close several centers around the State where first-year medical students were taught—including one in South Bend—and to bring all of medical education to Indianapolis, both to enhance its quality and to save money. But the chair of the State Senate Appropriations Committee was from South Bend, and he blocked the move.

During my first year I was talking with one State Representative about the University and its importance to the State, and he said to me, in essence, "Tom, you are a nice fellow, and I would like to help you. But until and unless I hear what you are saying from my own constituents, I am not going to support increased funding for the University." I realized then that we needed a real grass-roots campaign to gain that funding. With the Board's support, I used private donations to hire a Washington firm with expertise in grass-roots campaigning. Board members and I interviewed four firms before deciding on one with strong ties to Indiana as well as great political savvy.

The firm helped me organize "Hoosiers for Higher Education," which was a grass-roots group of Indiana University alumni and parents of University students, with a captain in each legislative district in the State. When the new legislative term was about to begin, the members of this new organization all came to the State Capital and fanned out to see their elected representatives. The effect was dramatic, and it kept building over the years I was there and is still a potent force today. Insofar as I know, this was the first such effort at any public university in the country.

I also was lucky to have advice from one of the giants in higher education, Herman B. Wells, who had been University president for more than 25 years, from 1937 to 1963, and was a legend when I arrived. He taught me, in his own words, "to dream great dreams," and to work with confidence to make them a reality. All through the early years of his presidency he kept in his desk plans of how the University could and should develop physically and academically, and he presided over the realization of those plans as the years went on, steering a small Midwestern college toward greatness. As one example, he supported the GI Bill, though it was opposed by Harvard President James Conant and other leading university presidents.

Wells was 84 when I first met him, and he quickly became my mentor in scores of situations. But it was the example of his leadership and his dedication to civic work that helped me far more than any individual insight during my own tenure. Most of all, Wells taught me to have high expectations about the University and public higher education. A scholarship program that bears his name is a wonderful illustration. When I came to Indiana University, I was troubled, as were others, that many of the best high-school students in Indiana were leaving the State for undergraduate education at leading institutions elsewhere. The University had worked hard to raise its admission standards, with some success. But the very best students—with few exceptions—still went elsewhere.

A new scholarship program, the Herman B. Wells Program, was designed to meet this challenge. High schools throughout the State were invited to nominate one or two of their best students for full full-tuition scholarships. Those nominated had to be not only academically outstanding students but well-rounded leaders as well. Fifty of the best nominees were invited to Bloomington for a weekend, much as outstanding football and basketball recruits come to be interviewed. Twenty-one were offered not only a full scholarship but also the opportunity to work closely with faculty members in their areas of particular interest.

The proposed Wells Scholarship Program faced a tough challenge in the Faculty Senate, because many of its members thought that a public university should only give scholarships based on need. I had sympathy for this position, but I thought that if the University was really to enhance undergraduate education, this program was needed. Fortunately, I had some allies who agreed with me that athletes should not be the only ones to receive financial aid without regard to need. But the key to success was when Herman B. Wells agreed to lend his name, for the first time, to the program.

I worried about how well the program would fare, for I realized that the young men and women offered the first Wells Scholarships were also offered scholarships at major private and public universities throughout the country. I knew the program would succeed, however, when 20 of the 21 high-school students chosen for the program accepted the scholarship. Even more important, some 200 applicants for the program who, our admissions director told me, would not have come to Indiana University otherwise, selected Indiana University even though they did not receive a Wells Scholarship. They chose the University because they wanted to come to an institution with high expectations, as signaled by the new program.

In the years that followed, I saw successive classes of Wells Scholars and was persuaded that the program raised expectations throughout undergraduate education at the University. I taught a seminar for Wells Scholars on philanthropy and public service, one of several courses that I taught while I was president. This one—for Wells Scholars—was particularly close to my mind and heart because it offered a chance for me to promote civic work as a career or an avocation among a group of students who were highly likely to be significant leaders in their communities.

The obvious corollary to the need for focus on a few key goals as a leader in civic work is the need to avoid distractions. I saw this in my work with George W. Ball when President Johnson was distracted from promoting his Great Society programs by the war in Vietnam.

In each of my subsequent civic work positions, I saw the potential for being distracted from my primary goals. This was strikingly true of those in leadership positions in higher education. When I was dean at Stanford Law School, for example, I watched as a fellow dean at Yale Law School was forced to resign because he and his wife spent School funds excessively on redecorating his office. But none of these experiences quite prepared me for the hailstorm of distraction I faced in my first year as Indiana University president over the University's basketball coach, Bob Knight, and his misbehavior.

The basketball team had won the NCAA championship the year before and Knight was riding high. He was Jekyll and Hyde, a remarkable mix of an abusive personality and a great teacher, a bully who was generous to the University library and many other good causes, and a foul-mouthed coach who was also steeped in knowledge of U.S. and military history. My predecessor had never sanctioned him, even when Knight threw a chair across the basketball court in a famous incident in Puerto Rico.

Like a little boy testing his parent, I immediately felt that Knight was testing me. I was only the second Indiana University president of his coaching career. We did not get off to a good start in the pre-season when he pulled his team off the basketball court in an exhibition game with a Russian team because he did not like the way the referees were handling the game. I made clear to him my view that when the University was involved in a public event, such a petulant performance was not acceptable.

An explosion came when Knight was being interviewed by a prominent TV commentator, Connie Chung. She talked with him on camera for several hours and used language as obscene as Knight's. At one point, in response to her comment, Knight said, "Well, it's like rape. If you can't avoid it, spread your legs and enjoy it." The comment was aired that night on national television, and I heard about it shortly thereafter. Thousands of calls came to my office from around the country condemning Knight and calling on me to fire him. The University faculty issued a resolution urging me to sanction Knight. In the next hour, I tried to reach Knight by phone to hear his side of the incident, but he was not available. So I made a public statement that sharply criticized Knight, stressed that his comment was unacceptable, and made clear that it was totally at odds with my own and the University's stance on behalf of promoting the dignity of women.

The next day, I heard through one of Knight's friends on campus that he was furious with me because I had not waited to hear his side before publicly condemning him. And, I was told, he was considering leaving the University for another coaching job. Within 24 hours, the story broke in newspapers around the country that Knight was being courted for the head coaching position at the University of New Mexico. Knight loved New Mexico and had suggested he might retire there someday, so the story seemed plausible. Within another day or two, he had flown to New Mexico to meet with the university president there and basketball backers who were eager to lure him.

All this made front page headlines in every newspaper in Indiana and was on the sports pages of papers throughout the country. I received over 10,000 letters and messages. The ones from within Indiana were overwhelmingly in favor of Knight and against me for sanctioning him. Those from elsewhere were just the reverse — and the further away from Indiana, the more likely it was that the writer would criticize Knight and support me. One letter I liked particularly was from rural Indiana and said, "I am an 85 year old woman who lives next to my TV set and loves Indiana basketball. You can take your God damn bow ties and go back East where you belong." I kept that letter in the top drawer of my desk and read it from time to time to remind me that Indiana

University belonged to the people of Indiana and not all of them would ever agree with my position on any particular issue.

For what I came to call "the six days of May," it was not clear whether Knight would go or stay. This was also the week of Indiana University commencements, and I flew in one of the two University planes each day to a different campus to lead the commencement ceremonies. At each campus, I was swarmed by reporters asking for comments. Governor Orr called me during one of the first of those days. "Tom," he said, "do you realize how serious this is? If Knight leaves, it could be disastrous for the State." I did not argue with the Governor, but simply said that I thought I understood the consequences.

During this week, I was still weighing what sanction, other than a public rebuke, I would impose on Knight for his outrageous comments. On the one hand, the comments were deeply objectionable to every decent-thinking person, and were particularly offensive to women. On the other hand, I was sure that if I imposed a harsh sanction such as suspension for a time, he almost certainly would leave. I had an academic agenda for the University that had been formed and was in the process of implementation. We had already attracted a number of new faculty to the University, and others were considering our offers. We had programs underway to strengthen undergraduate education, graduate education, research, and economic development in the State. I knew that if Knight left, this whole academic set of initiatives would be on hold for months, maybe years, because the State and the University would be in conflict about Knight. And I had already sanctioned him by the very harsh criticism I had stated publicly, something that had never happened to Knight before in all his years under my predecessor.

In the end, I concluded that it was wiser to do nothing further and to hope that Knight would stay at Indiana University. And, at the end of those six days in May, that is what he decided to do. Interestingly, like a bad boy who has tested his parents by stepping over the line of acceptable conduct, he never did so again while I was president. To the contrary, although he continued his foul language, his conduct was usually exemplary, and our relations became quite cordial. When my successor, Myles Brand, took over as president, however, the same pattern was reasserted, and ultimately Brand concluded he had to fire Knight. Unfortunately, Brand's own agenda for the University effectively came to a halt then, and he was unable to carry out many of the important initiatives that he had developed. Sometimes, of course, you must face and deal with a crisis even though it is not on your agenda as a leader, and Knight's behavior was one of those occasions for Brand, but the consequences for the larger goals of the University were disastrous, and Brandt soon decided that he needed to move to another job. Ironically, that position was as head of the NCAA.

When I became president of Indiana University in 1987, I was asked to join the Board of Campus Compact, and a few years later I was chosen as chair of the Board, a position I held until I resigned as Indiana University president in 1994. Initially, I along with others who were leading the organization thought that it would be enough simply to provide satisfying civic work opportunities for students. By 1990, however, it was clear to me that civic work would never be viewed by students or faculty as central to the mission of their institutions until it was integrated into the curriculum through what has come to be known as community-service learning. This is a pedagogy that links academic learning and civic work through structured reflection. This mode of active learning enables students to come to understand how they feel about what they think and how they think about what they feel.

In the years that followed, community-service learning became a major force in American higher education. It took time, however, until it became clear that in order to achieve learning outcomes that extend beyond academic learning to what Ernestine and I term "civic learning," care is needed in shaping the structured opportunities for reflection that link the academic and community experiences. Civic learning means coming to understand how a community functions, what problems it faces, the richness of its diversity, the need for individual commitments of time and energy to enhance community life, and most of all, the importance of working as a community to resolve community concerns.

In my years at Penn and particularly those at Indiana University, I thought extensively about how to promote civic work through civic learning. Initially, I did this through teaching community service learning courses at San Francisco State University, and helping create centers for community service-learning on the twenty-three campuses of the California State University (CSU) System, where I was a Distinguished University Scholar.

Soon after Ellen and I came back to California, I had the good fortune to connect with Lee Shulman, the new president of the Carnegie Foundation for the Advancement of Teaching. After five years teaching a variety of service-learning courses and building the network of centers on all the CSU campuses, I decided to accept Shulman's offer to join him at Carnegie and to write about civic issues. My luck was many times multiplied when someone whose work I much admired, Anne Colby, was asked to join the Carnegie Foundation as well, and we decided to work together.

Anne and I first connected because I used one of her books, *Some Do Care: Contemporary Lives of Moral Commitment* (Free Press, 1992), in the course that I taught for Wells Scholars when I was at Indiana University. I wrote her a fan letter, we met, and we worked together for the next eleven years at Carnegie. Anne, a superb psychologist of moral development, has spent her lifetime studying moral and civic development, primarily from her position as director of the Henry Murray Center at Radcliffe. Since I had spent much of my professional life in higher education and government service, we made a good team.

Over the course of my time at Carnegie, I edited one book on civic education, and Anne and I were co-authors of two others. Each of these works is focused on different aspects of how college students can gain the knowledge, skills, and attributes to be effective leaders in civic work. It has been one of the great pleasures of my professional life that I have been able to put into prose some of the insights that I learned in my civic work in the context of educating students.

ERNESTINE

I spent some time wondering what could I do to help other young people learn about entrepreneurship from an investor's perspective, a perspective I had acquired while working as an associate and Kauffman Fellow at Alsop Louie Partners. I found that perspective invaluable in deepening my understanding of entrepreneurship. My work in that realm has helped me immeasurably in my civic work, as I have indicated, and I wanted to assist would-be young entrepreneurs gain the knowledge and skills they would need, knowing that many would put them into practice in civic work as well.

Unfortunately, I frequently found, however, that senior entrepreneurs were dismissive of young entrepreneurs. An event for *Vanity Fair* magazine was a prime example. *Vanity Fair* had included me on its "Next Establishment List" for 2011, and the editors of the magazine were hosting an event at Monkey Bar in New York City to celebrate. I was excited to attend the event, as enthusiastic as when I had attended my first professional mixer at the Mackenzie Room and met Stewart Alsop, as I describe in Lesson 1. My positive mood quickly dampened, however, minutes after I entered the bar. What occurred next was, sadly, typical of what happens to many young people when they seek to engage in arenas where older people think that youth do not belong.

"So where do you live?" asked a middle-aged man. "At Stanford, in a college dorm," I responded.

His face then revealed that he thought I was just a kid who could not be seriously involved in the world of venture capital. The man promptly grabbed his wife's hand and darted off. I felt insulted, and at first, I could only sulk in the corner and feel sorry for myself. As I reflected on this experience, however, I soon realized how many older people had helped me in key phases of my life, including a number whose assistance is recounted in these pages, and this realization underscored my commitment to help empower young people to excel in whatever realm they might choose. And I affirmed to myself that I would never treat anyone of any age the way I had been treated at Monkey Bar.

Fortunately, through the Student Services Division of student government, which I had led, Stanford allows students to initiate new courses under the guidance of faculty members, and I was delighted when several professors in the Engineering school, including the dean of the Engineering School, James Plummer, agreed to speak at and support the course I had in mind. I knew that organizing the course would give me a sense of satisfaction in helping others to gain entrepreneurial skills as others had helped me.

When I started the class at Stanford during my junior year, I was amazed by how many people agreed to help. I remember how Bill Coleman would answer my emails within minutes after I sent them, how David Hornik would respond at even late hours in the night, and how Tom Kosnik would send me his comments at all hours. As an entrepreneur, Bill Coleman had co-founded BEA Systems, which under his leadership set the fastest record of any software company to reach a billion dollars of annual sales. As a lawyer, David Hornik had been a litigator in New York City at Cravath, Swaine & Moore, as well as an attorney representing high-technology startups such as Yahoo. And Tom Kosnik had taught entrepreneurship to MBAs, Ph.D.s, and undergraduates at Harvard and Stanford.

I was overwhelmed when all three individuals agreed to volunteer their time to serve on an advisory board to the class. They helped me shape the course, attended every single class session, and were seeming available every hour of the day. Bill, David, and Tom were unpaid volunteers in this civic work. I know they did this because they wanted to share with young people some of the wisdom they had gained over many decades of experience in entrepreneurship.

In addition to volunteering their own time, these three advisors helped recruit other entrepreneurs, venture capitalists, lawyers, and professors in Silicon Valley to serve as guest instructors for the course and as mentors for the students. Over ten weeks, the students met once a week for three hours to learn about entrepreneurship from experts in the field. Evan Williams, the co-founder of Twitter, for example, had played a significant role in shaping social media, and he held a wonderful roundtable discussion with the students. He talked about Twitter's role in the Arab Spring protest, and gave thoughtful responses to the suggestions of students about the potential future projects and goals of Twitter.

Our final class session was a chance for the students to meet informally with all the experts who had helped me during my career and provided advice that in turn shaped the course. Close to one hundred professionals who offered their expertise to the students were there, all actively engaged in talking to the students and providing further advice on issues such as gaining funding for new social-media projects. At the end of the session, everyone joined in a spirit of merriment, donning feather boas, top hats, and other fun props to pose with students at our makeshift photo booth.

The Silicon Valley leaders who helped in my course did not do so for any extrinsic reward. As I have felt in my own civic work, a sense of personal satisfaction in helping others was its own reward for them. "We are always happy to help people because it's good for the karma in the valley. Even though it sounds cheesy, it's something we all believe in," Jeff Clavier responded to a reporter who was also present at the event, when asked why he had helped in the course. Clavier is the founder of one of the first seed-stage venture-capital firms in the area, SoftTech VC.

My fellow State Farm® Youth Advisory Board member, Allante Nelson from Virginia, told me about what triggers his own inner sense of satisfaction in his civic work: when a smile lights up the face of a person in need whom he is assisting. He started volunteering at a battered-women's shelter when he was a student in middle school. Most of the women who stayed there had little or no income and were struggling to escape from an abusive relationship.

Allante told me about working with the children who accompanied the women in the shelter, and he particularly remembered one young girl named Page. He laughed as he told me about a game the children played called "Four Corners" because it used all four corners of the room. The children ran from corner to corner of the room on command, and when Allante told them to stop, those in each corner were supposed to act out a different activity. The group that finished first won the game. He said he could still see Page swinging her hands back and over her shoulders, bracing one foot in front of the other, swaying back and forth, then darting past the coloring table, into the far corner of the shelter. Like breaking a rack in a game of pocket billiards, she had started the game and the other children followed, whizzing through the room, dashing from corner to corner.

"Stop!" Allante commanded. Everyone froze. Page and those in her corner began hopping on one foot, giggling. Allante especially liked Page and the group of children that accompanied the women at the shelter. Most were only three or four years old and they seemed like perpetual motion machines. Whatever game Allante proposed, the children brought apparently tireless energy to playing it and, most important, they brought smiles. That's what meant the most to Allante: the children had the biggest smiles on their faces. Sometimes they seemed to be laughing so hard that their stomachs must have ached.

I remember a similar experience at the Shriner's Hospital for Children, a burn-treatment center in Los Angeles. A young girl was covered in gauze tape with her hair sticking straight up like pins, buzz-cut rather than flowing down, the way I liked my hair when I was her age. Her voice was raspy and cracked, like an old woman's. She had barely visible, colorless lips. Nonetheless, with her right hand perched on her hip, she threw her shoulder back, posing for the camera. Her other hand clutched my shoulder, and her face tilted toward mine. We looked as though we had been friends for years, although we had just met a few hours ago.

Through the early days of my life and civic journey, in working with "strangers" who suffer from difficult mental and physical disorders, I slowly gained a sense of understanding and ability to appreciate smiles as forms of thanks, as well as recognize different forms of personal fulfillment. But it took time to develop my sense of personal identity as enriched by my commonalities with others in need. When my peers and I began our community-service work through VAMS, we focused primarily on the many differences in circumstances between the people we were trying to serve and ourselves.

I remember first visiting Shriner's Hospital for Children in December of 2006 with my VAMS ensemble. Upon entering the center, my fellow volunteers and I saw some things we had never seen before: a large blue piece of cloth wrapped around a forearm; tape holding a thin plastic tube against a neck; and a white hospital gown with blue polka dots. My most vivid memory is of Anisha and a group of girls huddled in a corner. One of our high-school cheerleaders, Anisha had an almost perfectly proportioned face, long eyelashes that accented her eyes when she smiled, and lips that were usually shouting out encouragements. That day, however, rather than being her upbeat and peppy self, Anisha and her friends distanced themselves from the hospital patients. "What are we doing here?" I remember one saying, "This is scary."

One of many rewards I received through civic work was seeing the sharp line in my mind that marked these differences between us and the patients blur over time. We visited Shriner's Hospital for Children a few more times before I graduated from high school. Over time, I found that we had changed and gained a better understanding of the children whom we were serving and the challenges they faced every day. In the process, we developed ourselves and felt good about how we could relate to those in the world around us, whatever their challenges.

I remember that the cheeks of one young girl glistened from the topical gel smeared across her half-burned face. One of the young volunteers who worked with me at the hospital made her laugh by encouraging me to cover his cheeks in paint so that they could be "twins." Another patient's face was wrapped in white mesh, patched with thick pieces of gauze tape. Her volunteer "partner" wore a sparkly black top hat that almost hid his face and was covered with peppermints and candy canes. The lower right arm of a third young patient was missing, and a monochrome hospital bracelet adorned her other arm. Her volunteer "partner" was covered in vibrant mardi-gras beads up to his elbow. With these small gestures of empathy, we were able to bring smiles to the faces of those disabled children. Looking back, that was one of the best satisfactions of my civic work. It wasn't instantaneous. Rather, it happened over a few months. It was about transforming not just the audience for our music, but also ourselves.

Amanda Lim encountered a different set of challenges, yet was also able to redefine success and find her own form of satisfaction when she was a volunteer coach for the debate team at a high school in the middle of what those in Singapore call a "neighborhood school"—as contrasted with an "elite school." At one debate competition with teams from other schools, she watched in stunned amazement as she witnessed something she had never seen before, but nonetheless related closely to her own experiences. What she saw were tears gently flowing down the cheeks of one of the most confident team members, Bryant Tan. His head hung in uneasy shame. Four girls surrounded him, unsure of how to react, as they had never seen Bryant Tan shed a tear before. Just minutes before, crisply donned in a white collared shirt, denim jeans, and a red sports jacket, he had been rebutting the other team in a confident and articulate manner. His sudden shift shocked everyone in the room, particularly Amanda.

Bryant's discontented demeanor was all too familiar to Amanda because it was an attitude that she herself had experienced firsthand. He had the look of one who did not believe in himself anymore as he faced one of life's setbacks. Bryant was participating in a debate-style television show called *The Arena*, sponsored by Singapore's MediaCorp Channel 5. His team had just lost, and Amanda was reminded of the time that her high-school team had lost a national debate championship.

But unlike Amanda, Bryant came from a high school that did not have many resources or opportunities for extracurricular activities like debate. His debate team members had come a long way since Amanda had voluntarily decided to start coaching them just one year ago. Amanda had attended a high school that was in the top debate division. When she graduated from high school, she decided to help this school that was less fortunate.

Jurong Secondary School had not won a national debating title in the last ten years, and did not have the resources that Amanda's school did. Jurong Secondary School was unable to attract strong debate coaches, and every year, the school had fallen further and further behind. Emphasis was placed on other clubs and there was little incentive to foster a culture of excellence in debate. But ever since Amanda arrived to volunteer at Jurong, the team had made significant strides. They were now on a national television show, and this was their chance to shine. Or fail.

In the heat of debate, Bryant had made a coarse remark to his opponents, a comment that was condemned by the judges and audience, and this was precisely what the customarily confident boy was crying about. Amanda and I could both empathize with Bryant. From scoring poorly on an exam to watching a community-service event slowly fall apart, we had both often experienced that same feeling of loss and failure. Amanda shared these experiences with Bryant in a way that he will long remember. "It's okay to mess up," she said. "Everyone messes up. That's how we learn. Just remember to pick yourself up, and try again." Alok Vaid-Menon told me something along similar lines. In essence, he said that when you frame and focus on positives instead of negatives, everything seems like a winning situation, a reward. Several years down the road, when you look back, your stumble will seem like a small glitch in your otherwise successful life.

Looking back at my civic journey—a journey that I have only started—I see that my own civic work has evolved to include not only visiting hospitals and those in need through local organizations like VAMS, but also organizing philanthropy events, speaking on behalf of other nonprofit organizations seeking support, and promoting entrepreneurial ventures that value social and environmental benefits. Yet one common thread ties all these various experiences: a personal sense of satisfaction in trying to have a positive impact on the lives of others.

I recall a more recent event that occurred later in my time at Stanford—attending a clean-technology entrepreneurship event. I sat on a panel with three other investors—a partner at Mohr Davidow Venture, an early-stage funder at the angel investor fund, Band of Angels, and a director at Dow Jones. We had been invited to provide feedback to entrepreneurs seeking funding for their environmental business plans, and after spending around two hours at a conference center in San Jose, I was bombarded with questions, business cards, and requests for follow-up meetings from the audience of entrepreneurs.

Among the many requests for advice I had received at this event, like similar ones where I had been invited to speak, I heard few people say "thank you," apart from a couple via Twitter. When I finally left the San Jose conference center, a bit exhausted, I initially felt a bit misused. But then I realized, as I had so often in the past, that I had helped others who really needed reassurance and support, and that was my reward.

I have learned that it's difficult for many people even to accept that they require assistance, let alone to express gratitude for receiving aid. But if one keeps the broad aim of serving the public interest in mind when trying to help others, then thanks should not be needed, for civic work yields its own rewards in the sense of personal satisfaction that is gained and that becomes part of one's identity. Encountering difficulties is inevitable, but the results can be enormously rewarding because they provide the joy that comes in serving others and in realizing, once again, that we are all humans, bound together by our common humanity.

THE WAY FORWARD

Leveraging Technology for Civic Work

TOM AND ERNESTINE

In this last chapter we turn to the extraordinary set of opportunities for collaborative civic work by young people and others of all ages when they are aided by new technologies. For those in Ernestine's generation, using digital media generally, like YouTube, and social media like Twitter, Facebook, and LinkedIn, is as natural as using a pen or pencil. Tom and most of his generation have a harder time with these newer technologies as they grew up without them. His grandchildren are often his best teachers in this realm. Fortunately, each generation has important knowledge and skills that the other needs in terms of preparation for civic work.

As we discuss in this chapter, we have both witnessed how essential it is in civic work to combine traditional pedagogies with new technologies. We each believe that there is an urgent need now to help young people take an active lead in pressing the case for financing public education. Ernestine attended public schools until she came to Stanford University. Tom was president of one public university, Indiana University, and taught community-service-learning courses at another, San Francisco State University. Funding for these and other public educational institutions has been slashed in recent years and unless campaigns are organized to stop the slide into mediocrity of once-great public educational systems like those in California, the legacy will be crippling for generations to come.

Ernestine has been engaged in civic campaigns that leverage social media, and spells out four key steps—attract, engage, act, and measure—that are needed to make those campaigns successful, with examples of each step drawn from the stories of young people engaged in civic work. Tom has spent his entire career in education when not in government, and has organized campaigns to gain support for public education in the era before smartphones and Web 2.0. Both of us passionately believe that young people can and should partner with people of older generations in advocacy campaigns to promote vital public needs such as public education, and this chapter lays out the means for implementing these campaigns into reality.

TOM

Over the past decades, I have been involved in a number of national organizations whose purpose is to promote youth civic engagement. I have often thought that one or more of these organizations could provide a strong framework for youth to act collectively, particularly with a focus on issues that directly affect them and their future prospects for the kinds of lives they seek to live and the kind of world they want to live in.

I have already mentioned one of these organizations, Campus Compact, which was founded in 1985 and is now a national body with a membership of some 1,200 college and university presidents, and includes 34 state Campus Compact affiliates. While I was president of Indiana University, I served as the chair of the Campus Compact board, and in 1999, I helped draft a Declaration that has now been signed by hundreds of presidents from campuses across the country. That Declaration begins with these words:

> As presidents of colleges and universities, private and public, large
> and small, two-year and four-year, we challenge higher education to
> re-examine its public purposes and its commitments to the demo-
> cratic ideal. We also challenge higher education to become engaged,
> through actions and teaching, with its communities. We have a fun-
> damental task to renew our role as agents of our democracy. This

task is both urgent and long-term. There is growing evidence of disengagement of many Americans from the communal life of our society in general, and from the responsibilities of democracy in particular. We share a special concern about the disengagement of college students from democratic participation. A chorus of studies reveals that students are not connected to the larger purposes and aspirations of the American democracy. Voter turnout is low. Feelings that political participation will not make any difference are high. Added to this, there is a profound sense of cynicism and lack of trust in the political process.

Unfortunately, more than a decade later, the problems summarized in the Declaration are largely still with us. A major reason is that we have yet to find ways to empower America's youth to harness their energies and talents collectively to advocate for the public-policy changes that are needed and for them to act to ensure that their advocacy is not just empty rhetoric.

Campus Compact can play an important role in helping to break through the barriers to action by youth on key issues of public policy that directly affect their interests. Another organization with which I have been much involved can do so as well. This is the American Democracy Project (ADP), which includes some 240 public colleges and universities from across the country, all members of the American Association of State Colleges and Universities (AASCU). Together they represent more than one and a half million students.

Started in 2002, ADP has steadily evolved from a collection of institutions where civic learning was taking place on an episodic basis, largely formed around individual student civic volunteer activities, to a close-knit band of campuses that are helping each other grow stronger through multiple forms of civic education. More and more, we have seen that ADP members are promoting civic learning that goes beyond individual civic actions—actions to clean up a park, to tutor a kid, or to serve food at a community kitchen. ADP campuses are now educating their students to be politically engaged in their communities at every level: local, state, national, and international. By politically engaged, I mean involved in a full range of public-policy issues and not just partisan politics. We have seen that political engagement can be taught through a wide range of different academic disciplines: in the sciences, the social sciences, and humanistic fields, as well as vocational ones.

Anne Colby and I set out with two younger colleagues to write our book, *Educating for Democracy: Preparing Undergraduates for Responsible Political Engagement* (Jossey-Bass, 2007), about this form of teaching, because we found that it was severely undernourished on most campuses. George Mehaffy, the academic head of AASCU and the leader of the American Democracy Project, encouraged use of this book as a core text for ADP, just as he had championed our prior volume, *Educating Citizens: Preparing America's Undergraduates for Lives of Moral and Civic Responsibility* (Jossey-Bass, 2003), when ADP was founded. In the more recent book, we studied 21 strong courses and programs that we identified across the country that were teaching courses in various disciplines in ways that also integrated political engagement. A key finding of *Educating for Democracy* was that students in these courses and programs were not being pressured by their teachers to adopt particular ideological perspectives, but rather were encouraged to develop their own judgments across the entire ideological spectrum. In the years since we finished that volume, we have seen a significant rise in courses and programs that involve teaching students how to engage politically. Scores of articles and numerous books continue to be published examining various aspects of this development.

ADP has been continually evolving. Initially, it seemed remarkable that we could gain serious traction in promoting education for civic engagement in individual courses focused on the education of individual students. Today we not only see substantial programs across a range of fields designed to promote civic learning but entire institutions, guided by their presidents and provosts, have a dedicated commitment to ensure that their campuses are civic stewards of their communities. These programs ensure that students graduate as active, responsible, and knowledgeable civic leaders of their communities.

ADP is extraordinarily effective in terms of higher education. But what about K-12 schools? As Meira Levinson demonstrates in her powerful and persuasive book, *No Citizen Left Behind* (Harvard University Press, 2012), the need for civic education among K-12 school children is perhaps even more acute. I have been involved in two major programs to serve that end, though not as extensively as I have been engaged in civic learning for college students. One is a wonderful advocacy group called the Civic Mission of our Schools, which sponsors a national campaign to promote civic education in schools throughout the country. Former Supreme Court Justice Sandra Day O'Conner is helping to lead this program. The other organization is the Center for Civic Education, funded primarily by Congress, which operates in every state and Congressional district and sponsors a wide range of programs and curricular materials for schools to further the civic education of students. For a number of years, I served on its board.

These organizations are very much needed to promote civic education at every level. Today our country faces extraordinarily difficult civic problems, problems disguised as challenges, as my mentor, John W. Gardner, used to say. Many of the challenges seem to me ready-made for focused attention by groups such as these, for they directly impact today's youth and their future. The challenges include the dangers of climate change, the assaults on women's rights, the flood of money into politics, and many others that the youth mentioned in this book have sought to address. One stands out to me as a prime example: The cascade of body blows on the finances of public education at every level from pre-K through college and graduate education. We are all feeling the pain of this attack as public schools and colleges are reeling from devastating reductions in state support. How can educational institutions and their students help mobilize to respond effectively? I will use ADP as a case study to illustrate how because I have been particularly close to that organization. Nonetheless, my comments also apply to Campus Compact and other groups and every level of education.

I know the scene in California best. Its schools used to be the country's best. Now many are among the worst. The 23 campuses in the Cal State System, all members of ADP, are turning away well-qualified students and are relying increasingly on adjunct faculty, a troubling number of whom are itinerant teachers, shifting daily among three or even four campuses and paid at minimum wage or less. The California Master Plan, the great dream of Clark Kerr, is in tatters. I will not detail the disaster that lies ahead for our country as its once-vaulted education system is being decimated. Even those few states, such as Wyoming and North Dakota, that have so far avoided the crushing cuts that have become commonplace elsewhere, will feel the impact, for those states cannot flourish without neighbor states that have educated workforces and the systems of public schooling that are needed to prepare them.

What now can be done, acting collectively, to try to meet these challenges to our civic well-being generally, and particularly to combat the all-out assault on public funding for public education? My response is that we must turn to the tools of new technology that are so much a part of our students' lives, and help them use those tools in ways that will bring home to our citizenry the results of the civic crises we are facing.

Early in my tenure as Indiana University president, as I mention in Lesson 7, I set up a network of alumni supporters called Hoosiers for Higher Education. The program worked extremely well in terms of enhancing state support. And it is still going on today, many years after I left the University.

What we need now, I firmly believe, are counterpart campaigns that use new tools of technology to enable students, faculty, and staff to reach and influence state officials, particularly on behalf of adequate public funding for public education at every level. A study titled "Participatory Politics: New Media and Youth Political Action," led by Cathy J. Cohen of the University of Chicago and Joseph Kahne of Mills College provides strong evidence that young people from all backgrounds are increasingly using new technology tools for civic purposes.

I am not technologically savvy enough to design campaigns that employ these tools. Fortunately, my co-author, Ernestine, has thought deeply about the strategies that are needed to make maximum effective use of technology to promote civic work. I endorse her wise ideas with enthusiasm.

ERNESTINE

Technological development occurs in cycles during which new technologies displace existing ones. Each new cycle brings about changes in productivity, how people interact with the world, and our ability to connect with others. The advent of digital media is one such cycle. What we expected from the Internet in 2001, before YouTube, Facebook, LinkedIn, and Twitter, is very different than how we interact with it today. Over the next several decades, I can imagine new technologies that will have profound impacts on our abilities to engage in civic work. These technologies, for example, could print medical devices from 3D printers or expedite the distribution of relief materials to victims of natural disasters through autonomous navigation systems. A software company named Palantir Technologies, for example, partners with a nonprofit called Team Rubicon to provide disaster relief faster. The benefits of new technologies such as artificial intelligence, nanotechnology, and biotechnology will accelerate exponentially. As technologies improve, the benefits can help young people better connect to civic needs and enhance their productivity to meet those needs. Youth will need to learn to leverage these new technologies to enhance their civic work in meeting the increasing challenges the world will be facing in terms of food, water, energy, healthcare, and education. Youth will also need a strong public education in order to learn and leverage these technologies.

Digital media is a prime example of what I have in mind. I am constantly reminded of the power of digital media as I sit cross-legged in the second-floor computer cluster of my dorm, next to a computer with web browsers, documents, and other "windows" scattered across the screen. Social media particularly has greatly altered how people separated by space and time can still connect. The Arab Spring, for example, shows how activists in different Arab countries can use social media to come together, foster civic engagement, and bring about massive change.

What do "digital media" and "social media" mean? Digital media is the broader term and includes any form of electronic media in which data are stored in digital (as opposed to analog) form. Examples are websites, blogs, and emails. Social media, which is a subset of digital media, includes any digital-media form that allows for two or more people to interact, whether or not in real time. Facebook and LinkedIn are examples of social media that have become popular means to connect with networks of friends and colleagues. My tech-savvy friends almost always have one window on their computers open to the World Wide Web, displaying an arsenal of tools such as Gmail, Twitter, You-Tube, Wordpress, and Wikipedia, to name just a few. Next to their desktop or laptop, there will be a tablet open to even more windows and forms of digital media, as well as a smartphone or two with text messages from friends that span the globe.

Today's youth are highly digitally connected. For my generation, using technology seems perfectly natural: we have grown up with the World Wide Web and will have spent our entire lives with it. How can these tools be used to further civic work for this new generation of digital natives? One way to illustrate the answer is through my experiences with the State Farm® Youth Advisory Board, on which I served as a member for two and half years. As I previously mentioned, the Board gives five million dollars each year in grants to further social causes that youth lead and care about. These grants range in size from $25,000 to ones as large as $100,000. As a Board member, I usually leave a window on my computer open to the State Farm® Youth Advisory Board's fan page on Facebook.

In March 2012, my colleagues on the Board invited volunteers to submit online grants to what they termed the "Cause an Effect project." Volunteers from across the United States were encouraged to submit projects that would "cause an effect" in their local communities. Over the span of 20 days, about 3,000 proposals were received for projects. My fellow Board members reviewed the submissions and selected 100 finalists who had the most compelling projects. Facebook users then voted for their favorite projects, thus engaging the community directly in the funding process. This enabled communities to rally publicly behind causes that meant the most to them by voting on the State Farm® Facebook page, and the forty projects that received the most votes were then awarded $25,000 grants. Over 1.2 million votes were cast overall, with the top vote-getting cause receiving over 67,000 votes for its program alone. This example shows the power of digital media, and suggests how it might be used in the kind of youth campaign that Tom suggests in his section of this chapter. Digital media could enable a broad-based focus on a key public-policy issue of importance to youth such as adequate funding for public education at every level.

Having served on the Board for over two years before the online project was first implemented, I was able to see firsthand how digital media transformed a traditional grant-making process into an interactive online philanthropic outreach campaign. The result was a striking strengthening of civic work and engagement.

Initially, our applications involved lengthy documents and thus the process was slightly biased towards experienced grant writers such as teachers and administrators. The new digital-media approach allowed for a shorter, simpler process of submitting grants. Tapping into digital media and hosting the program on Facebook made the entire application process user-friendly, quick, and easy to complete. With shorter grant applications, our applicant demographic changed. We expanded beyond our typical audiences and were able to engage with entire communities that may not have been familiar with the traditional grant process. More volunteers were able to become involved in the grant-writing process. Digital media helped bring to a much wider audience the opportunities that the Board was providing.

This new way of funding grants provided the Board with a level of engagement and publicity that its members had never seen before. Our Facebook page traffic increased enormously. Over half of the applicants had heard about the program through social media, with 37% through Facebook and 21% through other websites.

As this example illustrates, digital media has great benefits. But it also has several limitations. The new "Cause an Effect" program made it harder to select the best grants because the online applications provided much less information, as my fellow board member Alex Wirth told me. As a consequence, the Board found that the more traditional methods, involving lengthy applications, still were needed when applicants were seeking large grants of more than $25,000. The Board has since adopted a hybrid method for distributing funds, using traditional grant applications for larger grants, as well as online grant applications for smaller ones.

The "Cause an Effect" grant project is just one example of using social media to promote civic work. With that example in mind, we can consider how new technology might be employed to promote other aspects of civic work.

I went to a public high school in Los Angeles and experienced first hand the impact of budget cuts in education across the state of California. A number of teachers and administrators, including the music teacher who sponsored my nonprofit organization VAMS, circled in and out of the school, as they were hired and fired. Tom mentions the public Cal State system and the California Master Plan, and I wholeheartedly agree that a major national issue such as funding for public education at all levels could benefit from a youth civic campaign that uses digital media. This is an ideal illustration of the kind of national public-policy problem that youth can use digital media generally, and social media particularly, to help promote needed reforms. Four key steps should be followed to enhance civic work by using these existing technologies — and other new technologies that will emerge in the years ahead. These steps are: Attract, Engage, Act, and Measure.

Attract

First, you need to attract a target audience. That means thinking hard about why that audience would want to join your cause. How will you brand and position the cause? How will you grab attention with a compelling story that connects you with your target group? A campaign will need the counterpart of a story like that of a young civic star Tom and I interviewed named Travis Kiefer. Travis gained national recognition when he decided to take a temporary leave from Stanford and raise money for a nonprofit he started for micro-lending in developing countries. Within one year, he secured several thousand dollars, all in small micro-donations. How did Travis—almost single-handedly—raise all that money?

Travis believed passionately that micro-lending was essential for third-world development and wanted to raise funds for that purpose. But how was he to do that with no funds himself? One of his friends, a health-advocate, thought Travis should begin exercising and told him, "I'll give you $5 if you start running." Travis was never much of a runner, but his friend encouraged him. Through this peer's inspiration, Travis decided to drag a treadmill into the cafeteria meat locker at Stanford and begin jogging. As he ran farther and farther, he had a new goal: to run a marathon on every continent and raise micro-donations for his micro-lending nonprofit, called Gumball Capital, while doing so. And in soliciting donations, he wanted to add a compelling, personal touch: to make personal videos during the runs for anyone who donated at least $25.

Travis ran marathons in Ireland, Argentina, Japan, San Francisco, Zimbabwe, and Australia, making hundreds of videos along the way. His fundraiser gained new momentum a few days before he headed off to the South Pole—Antarctica. A web publication called *TechCrunch* picked up Travis's odyssey and featured him on its homepage. Like many other students at Stanford, I heard about Travis's story when it was virally shared on multiple digital-media sites, first through my network at Stanford, and then much more widely. Travis and his story charmed thousands of other people across the United States. Moreover, the article referred to Gumball Capital's website, and the organization's website traffic spiked up to 10,000 people visiting within two days after the article was written. Within a short time, Travis raised enough money to operate Gumball Capital for a year. Travis had a compelling saga that drew interest and publicity, and most important, it attracted financial contributions.

To gain supporters, in addition to having a compelling story, brand consistency is key. Successful organizations have distinct brands that are highly recognizable. Change.org, for example, has a clear, targeted message: "to empower anyone, anywhere to start, join, and win campaigns for social change." This well-defined message of promoting social change through the use of online petitions has enabled millions of people to create and sign online petitions, ranging from one that encouraged Universal Studios to update its website to reflect environmental concerns, to one that urged Bank of America and subsequently President Obama to examine out-of-control banking fees. In attracting its supporters, Change.org maintains its brand consistency. Other successful online organizations have similarly distinct brands.

In addition to having a compelling story and consistent brand, I have learned that there are many "do not's" in using social media to attract supporters. "Do not bombard your supporters," is one key lesson I learned. Sending a message every six hours dissipates its impact. "Do not post items that are irrelevant to your cause or that do not fit your demographics," and "Do not use social media without considering more traditional approaches," are two other lessons I have learned. We need to keep these in mind as well as the affirmative case that must be made.

Engage

A compelling story is essential to grab attention, and Travis's saga had a compelling power that engaged people. But that's only the first step.

Travis was able to build up great enthusiasm during his initial efforts, and Gumball Capital had the proper web servers in place to accommodate a spike in web traffic as a result of those efforts. But this enthusiasm could not be sustained because of lack of funds. Unfortunately, the organization lacked a strong board of directors to help lead the needed fundraising and Travis could not do that on his own given all the other challenges of running the organization. As a result, Gumball Capital was disbanded two years later. In hindsight, we can learn that you must not only locate key financial contributors at the outset, but also find those who can help identify other new donors in a widening circle of support so that each financial contribution makes the next one more likely. In this process, it is important to engage donors in your cause in ways that make them feel they are not just financial backers, but also real participants in helping to further the organization's goals.

Once you attract your target audience, you must earn the trust of those you contact and keep them engaged, preferably before you call for action. Audience engagement can be promoted in numerous ways, such as encouraging collaboration and debate, using an incentive program, and generating the right graphic tone in your online materials. In employing these approaches, it is always useful to seek counsel from your supporters: ask them what they want, rather than just doing what you want.

One great strength of social media is that it can promote collaboration and debate. Tom wrote his senior thesis at Harvard on the role of public opinion in our democracy over a half century ago, when public opinion polling was just becoming a professional undertaking. It is infinitely more reliable today. But it is not tapping public opinion that can transform new generations of our citizenry from spectators to knowledgeable citizens engaged in civic work. Rather, that transformation occurs when they interact with each other and with public officials around key issues, and this can happen with the aid of social media far more deeply than has ever been feasible before.

A prime example is the way Professor Rob Reich of Stanford uses Facebook to promote deep discussions among his students. As one illustration, he posted a short article questioning why more Stanford students entered finance and management consulting, rather than other sectors. Within a few hours, both current and recent Stanford students gave their reactions, leaving often lengthy postings. By the end of the day, over fifty students had commented, and the Facebook discussion eventually led to a column in *The New York Times* by David Brooks. Social media, when triggered by such a thoughtful prompt, can be an effective means to promote deep dialogues that can earn the trust of supporters from across time and space. The lesson is clear: Social media allows you to engage people in ways we could have never dreamed of previously. Before you ask volunteers to sign your petition or donate, use social media to engage them.

A key strength of social media is that you do not have to stick to traditional black and white letters. Your message does not have to be just text; you can use images, videos, and an array of social outlets to convey emotional stories in a different way, as my friends Kevin Mo, Victor Em, and Vineet Singal did through Stanford Professor Jennifer Aaker's 100K Cheeks Challenge for bone-marrow drives. In an effort to swab cheeks, expand the bone-marrow drive registry, and thereby match potential donors for bone-marrow transplants to those with leukemia, my colleagues combined traditional means of volunteering with a new online visual atmosphere. I remember passing by White Plaza in the center of Stanford's campus during their campaign period. A few dozen signatures and bags of cotton soaked in saliva were piled on a table. Kevin's left hand grasped a stack of bulky signs. "Swab a cheek. Save a life." "Are you my type?" "10 minutes can save a life." Victor's hands rapidly tapped his iPhone, snapping photos and instantly posting them, one by one, to Facebook. Vineet's right hand guided volunteers as they clutched one of the thin plastic sticks tipped with cotton, while his left grasped three other cotton swabs. Forcing his mouth wide open, he swabbed his inner cheek twice. Mouth still agape, somewhat awkwardly posed, and elbow bent, he went through the other swabs in a similar fashion. Over the next few hours, more and more students also swabbed their cheeks. And Victor snapped more and more photos.

At the end of the day, lunch remained perfectly wrapped, unopened. The list of names and signatures and the pile of used cotton swabs had grown though. So had the virtual stack of photos Victor and his fellow volunteers had taken. The volunteers posted these photos on their individual Facebook pages. They had excellent sets of photos that could also be shared on community pages, photo-sharing websites, and even paper flyers. How do photos and social media promote civic work? Often, it helps just to see a picture of young people engaged in civic work. Photos shared through social media connect people and encourage them to become engaged. They help generate the right visual atmosphere and allow viewers to think visually and in color.

Another key lesson in promoting a conversation through social media is using collaboration between social sites to ensure sharing and scale. For example, a blog and Twitter post should not be viewed as separate tools, but rather it can be effective to "tweet" blog posts and include a blog link that encourages readers to "follow" you on Twitter. The maximum impact comes by taking a holistic perspective. At the same time, in using various forms of social media, it is rarely wise to duplicate content on these different social-media outlets. For example, Twitter posts should not be the same as Facebook posts. Think of Twitter as an opportunity for short bits of text and news, while Facebook can allow an audience to comment directly on posts and engage through in-depth conversations. Conversation and visual interaction, coupled with trust, can allow you to engage and understand your audience better than would otherwise be possible.

Act

"Viral buzz" is great, but when you have that, the party isn't over. It's only begun. Once you attract and understand an audience, you need to build on your audience's enthusiasm. Turn passion into action. You will need to transform collective advocacy into civic action. Otherwise, you are stuck with casual support, and your so-called supporters will not be actively engaged. I was able to leverage social media and turn passion into action when recruiting volunteers for my nonprofit VAMS.

The summer after my freshman year at Stanford, I returned home to Los Angeles. Having left Southern California for college at Stanford in Northern California, I had been physically distanced from VAMS for quite a few months. I was, in fact, 380 miles away. Returning to Los Angeles that summer brought back memories, reconnecting with old friends and volunteers, cruising the streets of San Fernando Valley, and most enjoyably, hanging out by the pool and catching up with my sister Christine.

With the help of my sister, I decided to launch a summer internship program for VAMS. However, since graduating high school in Los Angeles, leaving the birthplace and headquarters of VAMS, and subsequently placing the nonprofit in the hands of other actively-involved students and volunteers at my high school, I was separated from the organization in terms of distance, although VAMS remained close to my heart.

I had an action item: I wanted to recruit new volunteers who would serve as summer interns to help grow the organization. Although far away from where my nonprofit had started, I leveraged the power of social media and employed a wide range of social-media tools to encourage action. Some of the strategies I adopted included writing blog posts, messaging friends and volunteers on Facebook, and posting on an online platform for social change called VolunteerMatch.org.

Through social media, I was able to recruit students from across the United States: a fellow civic leader at Stanford; an active VAMS volunteer across the Bay at University of California, Berkeley; a local high-school student a bit farther away in Fremont, California; and other young high school and college students from across the country—including some in Minnesota, Illinois, and Massachusetts. These volunteers all had access to the Internet, were able to work remotely, and they devoted their summers to volunteering for VAMS.

The following summer further verified the power of social media. For the first time, I was able to direct volunteers outside of our immediate VAMS network. I was thrilled that dozens of students applied. As I traveled and took "red eye" flights from Florida to Oklahoma, hopping from hotel to hotel for a summer engineering internship, and even living in northern Alaska for a few weeks, Armand Ontiveros and Eileen Ung helped me direct the volunteers. Armand was a fellow board member with whom I worked on the State Farm® Youth Advisory Board. Eileen was a fellow Stanford student who had worked under me for the Student Services Division arm of student government. Armand lived in Illinois, Eileen remained in Northern California, and I traveled across the United States.

As I lived out of a suitcase, I constantly leveraged the strengths of the Internet and social media. Slouched over the hard, somewhat uncomfortable chairs in airports, I was able to respond to emails through my Blackberry and communicate with my fellow internship directors over Skype on my iPad. The power of technology enabled me to add new volunteers and supporters and remain connected with people from around the world.

At the same time, we continued to pursue traditional methods of volunteering. At the end of the summer, we brought together a group of summer volunteers in Los Angeles to Chevy's Restaurant, and I was reminded of the power of being able to connect or reconnect with people in person. I met with former high school volunteers and Mr. Rodriguez, who had been so helpful to me when I started VAMS. As we finished eating corn tortillas and sipping on horchata soft drinks, one volunteer turned to me, "Ernestine, keep in touch," he said, "Facebook!" We have since kept in touch through social media. The power of the Internet is incredible and does not replace meeting someone face-to-face. Nonetheless, it is a convenient and powerful way to maintain and strengthen relationships when people are separated by many miles or oceans.

Measure

Finally, measuring is a critical step in using social media to promote civic engagement. Had I measured the progress of VAMS more actively, the organization might have been more successful. One of the biggest challenges faced by civic causes, particularly those led by young people, is maintaining the organization on a growth curve once the founder leaves. Membership rapidly decreased when I left VAMS, and several chapters even shut down. Had I remained actively engaged through technology, I might have been able to track my nonprofit's progress better, keep volunteers more engaged, and assist more promptly and effectively when issues arose.

I cannot stress how important it is to measure results. Far too often, organizations do not spend enough time to reflect and measure how well they are succeeding. That being said, social listening tools and analytics allow you to measure effectiveness and identify areas of improvement. This is a key and critical last step. These tools can be used to measure, collect, and analyze historic data to determine the most appropriate themes to highlight and paths to promote.

In evaluating success, as I have come to realize, you must first set appropriate key performance indicators, which will depend on what is important to the organization. These metrics can be measured through quantitative or qualitative means, or a combination of both.

Quantitative indicators are sometimes available to allow success to be presented numerically. In the world of social media, Facebook users can interact with material in one of three ways: "like," "share," or "comment." "Liking" requires the least amount of effort as it involves simply clicking a button; "sharing" entails reposting another person's message; while "commenting" requires the most time and thought. "Insights," just one Facebook tool for measuring success, allows you to quantify each of these three interactions and compare the number of times someone has viewed a post to how often that person has taken action. Other quantitative metrics include the number of times a page is viewed, how much money is generated, and how many people are helped.

The realm of social media also has qualitative methods for better understanding volunteer behavior and the reasoning behind such behavior. Google Alerts, for example, is a service that uses real-time listening tools to hear and understand what is immediately being discussed through blogs, videos, news, and other web content. Combined, both quantitative and qualitative indicators can help us measure success in using social media.

The State Farm® Youth Advisory Board, for example, was able to measure results from the "Cause an Effect" online grant campaign. They showed how submitters heard about the program: 1,114 through Facebook, 635 through other websites, 546 through State Farm® agents, and 156 via word of mouth. They found out who submitted causes: the youngest person was 13, while the oldest was 88. They told us that in response to the call for proposals, the average was more than 13 submissions per hour, and that the goal of 500 submissions had been surpassed on day four. And they pinpointed exactly where submissions came from. At the same time, program coordinator and former Board member Brad Corriher shared with me, "The most important measurements are still about the impact that these grants will have on communities, and our ability to raise awareness of the great work that the Youth Advisory Board does."

As I glance at my laptop and return to a window open to Facebook, I see posts from former high-school teachers. Mr. Maine was one teacher, who, like Rob Reich, used Facebook to inform both current students and alumni of the problems North Hollywood High School faced. He frequently shared articles discussing the limited access to textbooks, the decline in qualified teachers, and the lack of effective curricula that promoted adaptive learning. California's overall system of education now ranks near the bottom of all states.

While saddened that many of the teachers who had supported me in high school are now struggling from state-wide budget cuts in public education, I am nonetheless able to remain informed of the situation through social media. I am not only educated by social media, but also empowered by my ability to communicate with others to help in a campaign to build support.

We face the challenge of crafting a message that makes evident the disastrous consequences if public-education funding continues to evaporate. This requires us to understand our target audience, as too often our citizenry see public education as though it were solely a private good to meet the vocational needs of students. But the education organizations Tom discussed in this chapter were all founded on the bedrock principle that young people should be educated to be knowledgeable, responsible, and actively engaged in the civic lives of their communities. Over the past decade, we have seen that this message resonates well with students and their families if it is stated in a vigorous, compelling manner, not as some fluffy afterthought that uses gaining employment as the only rationale for public education.

We can make existing civic education and engagement efforts more student and citizen centered by using new technology such as digital media. We can make organizations such as ADP more interactive and participative. We can harness new technologies to engage more students, and to make our teaching and programming more effective. I am confident that youth can play major roles as civic leaders in meeting the public-policy challenges in education and other arenas, and that their roles must involve effective uses of new technologies.

TOM AND ERNESTINE

Freshmen at Stanford in the late 1920s and '30s were required to take a year-long course called "Problems of Citizenship." The course was one-fourth of the normal first-year undergraduate curriculum, and was rooted in the judgments of the University's founders, Jane and Leland Stanford, that education for civic leadership should be a primary goal of an undergraduate education. In the words of Mrs. Stanford, "While the instruction offered must be such as will qualify the students for personal success and direct usefulness in life, they should understand that it is offered in the hope and trust that they will become thereby of greater service to the public."

In the opening lecture in 1928, the first year the course was offered, Professor Edgar Eugene Robinson told students "citizenship is the second calling of every man and woman. You will observe as we go forward that our constant endeavor will be to relate what we do and say to the facts of the world from which you came and in which all of you will live, and to correlate the various aspects of the modern scene, so that it will appear that citizenship is not a thing apart, something to be thought of only occasionally or left to the energies of a minority of our people, but that its proper understanding is at the very root of our daily life."*

We both believe that Jane Stanford was right. Young people have an obligation to engage in civic work that will benefit their communities. In the decades since Jane and Leland Stanford founded Stanford University, the planet has shrunk so that those communities include not just places in our immediate vicinity, but throughout the entire world. The stories in this book reveal just how powerful an impact young people can have in their civic work, whatever the size and location of the communities they serve.

Education for civic leadership is no longer part of the formal curricula of Stanford and most other colleges and universities. Civics, which used to be a regular course in elementary schools, and often in secondary schools as well, has virtually disappeared from their curricula. Students learn about public affairs, but rarely do they learn how to engage in promoting sound public policies on the local, state, national, and international levels. As we have seen, however, youth throughout the country are engaged in extraordinary civic work that enhances the lives of people in need and gives those young people a sense of personal satisfaction that shapes their very identity. The lessons we suggest in this book to promote civic work are not difficult to learn, though the work itself is rarely easy. The challenges can often be daunting, as some of the experiences we have recounted make clear.

Over time, and with practice, we know that civic work can become for young people an essential part of their identity, of who they are and how they relate to the world around them and to those in need. This shaping of character is the journey of a lifetime, one that never ends. We hope that our words, which reflect our own experiences, make the road clearer and its rewards more inviting.

NOTE

*The story of the Stanford course on Problems of Citizenship and the related quotations are based on Chapter VI in W.B. Carnochan, *The*

Battleground of the Curriculum (Stanford University Press, 1993). Professor Robinson's first lecture in the course is reproduced in the appendix to that book. Tom has used this story in prior publications.

ACKNOWLEDGMENTS

We gratefully acknowledge the support of those who gave us wise counsel in writing this book. They include: Blaine Chatman, Anne Colby, Mary Huber, Pat Hutchings, David Mathews, Kim Meredith, and Jasmine Schladen.

INDEX

Commission on National and Community
Service, 65
Committee on Land and Buildings, 49, 50
community-service learning, 135–136;
funding decrease, 145
Conner, Kimberly (Stanford student),
114–116
Corbett, Alf, 103
Corporation for National and Community
Service, 14
Corriher, Brad, 161
Costello, Frank ("the Prime Minister of
the Underworld"), 8
Court of Appeals, U.S., 107
craftsmanship, 6, 7–8, 11
Crampton, Roger, 78, 79, 80, 81, 82
Cromwell, Oliver, 9
Crowell, Bill, 21
Crown, Henry (Stanford donor), 102
Crown Quadrangle, 102
CSF. See California Scholarship
Federation
CSU. See California State University
Cuban Missile Crisis, 23–24; quarantine
debate, 25–26; working for Chayes
during, 25–28
Cummins Engine, 129
Curley, James Michael, 64

debate: competition, 141–142; through
social media, 156–157
Declaration, Campus Compact, 146–147
Declaration of Independence, 3
Delek Hospital, 92–94; McCullough as
doctor at, 94–95; Tibetan refugee
patient, 93–94
Democratic Club, 64
Democratic Party, campaigning for, 32.
See also American Democracy Project
Department of Agriculture, 121
Diem, Ngo Dinh, 85
digital media, 151–153; definition, 151;
public-policy problem and, 153
disaster-relief technology, 150
dispassionate objectivity, 9
Distinguished University Scholar, 135
Dominican Republic, U.S. invasion of, 28
DoSomething.org, 52
Dow Jones, 142

Draper, Bill, 20
Draper Richards Kaplan Foundation, 20
Draper Richards LP, 20
The Duke's Children (Trollope), 75

East Palo Alto community, 90
*Educating Citizens: Preparing America's
Undergraduates for Lives of Moral and
civic Responsibility* (Colby/Ehrlich),
61, 148
*Educating for Democracy: Preparing
Undergraduates for Responsible
Political Engagement* (Colby/Ehrlich),
148
education: civic leadership, 163; civic
work and, 59–60; funding for public,
149–150, 162. *See also* civic education
Ehrlich, Elizabeth (daughter), xvii
Ehrlich, Ellen (Tom's wife), xv, 128; civic
work of, 61; Harriman and, 124; leak
to reporters by, 45
Ehrlich, Tom: books co-authored with
Colby, 61, 148; early career choices
and motives, 62–67; father of, 5;
international law treatise co-authored
by, 28; as Jew, 127, 129; mother of,
3–4, 5, 60–61
elections, 31; 2000 presidential, 31
The Elements of Style (Strunk/White), 44
empathy, 92, 141
Enad, Racquel (Visayan intern), 37–39
Endeavor Global, 109
engage step, 155–157
entrepreneurship, 109; civic work and, 17;
clean-technology, 142–143; teaching
youth about, 17, 137–138; youth
viewed by senior entrepreneurs,
17–137
Ernestine. *See* Fu, Ernestine
Ewing Marion Kauffman Foundation,
109. *See also* Kauffman Fellows
Program
Exeter Academy, 59
expectations, of gratitude, 118, 123, 128

Facebook, 152, 156, 158
father, Tom's, 5
Federal Bureau of Investigation (FBI),
120

ABOUT THE AUTHORS

Thomas Ehrlich has held a number of public-service positions since the administration of President John F. Kennedy. He was the first head of the Legal Services Corporation and was the director of the agency responsible for foreign-aid policy, reporting directly to President Carter. He has also served as president of Indiana University, provost of the University of Pennsylvania, and dean of Stanford Law School. He is author, co-author, or editor of fourteen books, including *Educating Citizen: Preparing America's Undergraduates for Lives of Moral and Civic Responsibility* (2003), and *Educating for Democracy: Preparing Undergraduates for Responsible Political Engagement* (2007). He has received five honorary degrees and is a member of the American Academy of Arts and Sciences.

Ernestine Fu is an undergraduate student at Stanford, where she has been admitted to the Master's and PhD programs in engineering. She has been engaged in civic work since she was fifteen when she founded a nonprofit organization to bring music to those in need. She has served on a national corporate advisory board to fund youth civic activities. She had also worked at a venture capital firm emphasizing investments in high-tech Silicon Valley start-ups. She was chosen for the Kauffman Fellowship on entrepreneurship and is an active supporter of social entrepreneurs.